Software Architect

Mahbouba Gharbi is managing director and Chief Architect at ITech Progress GmbH, and chairman of the board at the International Software Architecture Qualification Board (iSAQB). She is a self-confessed software architecture enthusiast and the author of many expert articles. She is a welcome guest speaker at numerous international conferences.

Prof. Dr. Arne Koschel is a lecturer at the University of Applied Sciences and Arts, Hannover, Germany specializing in distributed (information) systems. He has many years of industry experience planning and developing distributed information systems. His lectures include a broad range of IT topics, including cloud computing, integration, middleware, microservices, and SOA. He is an active member of the iSAQB board.

Prof. Dr. Andreas Rausch is head of the software systems department at the Technical University of Clausthal. He is a consultant and lead software architect for a number of large-scale distributed software systems.

Mahbouba Gharbi · Arne Koschel · Andreas Rausch

Software Architecture Fundamentals

A Study Guide for the Certified Professional for Software Architecture®

- **Foundation Level**
- **iSAQB compliant**

Content proofreading by Andrew Le Gear

 dpunkt.verlag

Mahbouba Gharbi · m.gharbi@itech-progress.com

Arne Koschel · akoschel@acm.org

Andreas Rausch · andreas.rausch@tu-clausthal.de

Editor: Michael Barabas / Christa Preisendanz
Content proofreading: Andrew Le Gear
Copyeditor: Jeremy Cloot
Layout and type: Josef Hegele
Cover design: Helmut Kraus, www.exclam.de

Library of Congress Control Number: 2019931449

Bibliografische Information der Deutschen Nationalbibliothek
Die Deutsche Nationalbibliothek verzeichnet diese Publikation in der Deutschen
Nationalbibliografie; detaillierte bibliografische Daten sind im Internet über http://dnb.d-nb.de
abrufbar.
978-3-86490-625-1

Copyright © 2019 dpunkt.verlag GmbH
Wieblinger Weg 17
69123 Heidelberg

Title of the German original: Basiswissen für Softwarearchitekten.
Aus- und Weiterbildung nach iSAQB-Standard zum Certified Professional for Software
Architecture – Foundation Level.
3., überarb. u. akt. Auflage 2018
ISBN 978-3-86490-499-8

Preface

In addition to motivated teams and great management, software architecture is an important factor for the success of any software project. In the context of systematic design and construction, solid software architecture ensures the fulfilment of quality requirements such as extensibility, flexibility, performance, and time-to-market.

Software architects reconcile customer requirements with the available technical options and the prevailing conditions and constraints. They ensure the creation of appropriate structures and smooth interaction of all system components. As team players, they work closely with software developers and other parties involved in the project.

The International Software Architecture Qualification Board (iSAQB) is an independent international body that defines standards for training, examination, and certification of software architects. **Software Architecture Fundamentals** is based on the curriculum for the iSAQB's *Certified Professional for Software Architecture – Foundation Level (CPSA-F)* course.

The text is based on the revised version 4.1.1 of the curriculum, which has been expanded to cover new aspects of domain-driven design (DDD). DDD enables software architects to design large-scale functional structures and gain a better understanding of the overall interaction of functional components. The current curriculum also covers numerous new architectural patterns such as microservices.

CPSA-F certification ensures that software architects have sound levels of knowledge and expertise for the design of small and medium-sized systems. Based on a detailed requirements specification, they can then design and document appropriate software architectures. CPSA-F graduates have the requisite skills for making problem-specific design decisions that build on their previous practical experience.

This self-study book enables you to prepare for the certification examination. It assumes that you have practical experience designing and developing software systems, command of a high-level programming language, and an understanding of the basics of UML. Because lectures alone cannot replace interaction with other software architects, we also recommend participation at iSAQB attendance-based events.

Benefit from our many years of experience in software and systems engineering, and in the design and construction of medium- and large-scale IT systems.

We hope you enjoy reading our book and wish you every success with your CPSA-F training and certification!

Mahbouba Gharbi, Arne Koschel, Andreas Rausch
December 2018

Content

Appendix

Table of Contents

Appendix

1 Introduction

Nowadays, software is everywhere, from commercial enterprises to virtually all areas of our day-to-day professional, public, and private lives. Air travel, phone calls, bank transfers, or driving would all be next to impossible without software. Software-controlled components can be found in every home and in many everyday devices, from washing machines to cars [BJ+06]. Software is not usually autonomous, but is instead embedded along with hardware and electronics, or as part of the business processes that companies use to generate value [TT+00].

The value and commercial success of companies and products is increasingly determined by software and software quality (see [BM00], [SV99], [TT+00]). Software engineers are thus faced with the challenge of implementing increasingly complex requirements at ever-increasing speed using ever-decreasing budgets while maintaining a high level of software quality.

Continual increase in the size and complexity of software systems has made them some of the most complex human-made systems ever created. The best example is the Internet, which is a truly global software-based system. Internet is now available beyond the bounds of our home planet on the International Space Station (ISS).

A structured and systematic approach to design is essential for the success of software-based systems. Despite the use of established software development methods, the number of unsuccessful software projects remains alarmingly large. To counter this, we need to avoid as many errors as possible, or identify and eliminate them during the early phases of software engineering. Requirements engineering and software architecture are two of these phases. In the words of Ernst Denert, one of the fathers of methodical software development, software architecture is the "Ultimate software engineering discipline" (taken from Denert's foreword in [Sie04]).

1.1   Software architecture as an aspect of software engineering

Problems with software projects were identified as early as the 1960s, and were referred to then as *"the software crisis"*. From 7–11 October 1968, the NATO Science Committee invited 62 internationally renowned researchers and experts to a conference in Garmisch, Germany, to address the future of software development. This conference is now regarded as the birth of modern software engineering [Dij72].

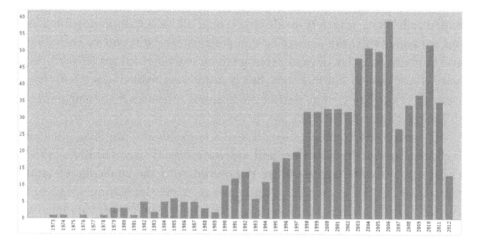

Figure 1-1   *Publications on the subject of software architecture since 1973 [Reu12]*

Compared to traditional engineering disciplines (such as construction) that can fall back on several thousand years of experience, software engineering is still an extremely young discipline. It is therefore no surprise that the sub-discipline of software architecture is even younger. Figure 1-1 shows an increasing number of publications on the subject of software architecture from the 1990s onward [Reu12]. These figures are taken from *The Web of Knowledge*—one of the largest and most renowned publication databases.

With a view to the long history of construction architecture, Marcus Vitruvius Pollio (a Roman architect from the first century BC) was an architectural pioneer. In *De architecture*—nowadays known as *Ten Books on Architecture* [Vit60]—he argued that good architecture can be achieved using a clever combination of the following elements:

Utilitas (usefulness):
The building performs its function.

Firmitas (solidity):
The building is stable and long-lasting.

Venustas (elegance):
The building is aesthetically pleasing.

Figure 1-2   *Architecture in ancient Rome*

This hypothesis can be directly applied to the discipline of software architecture. The objective of software architecture (and thus a software architect's primary task) is to construct a system that balances the following three attributes:

Utilitas (usefulness):
The software fulfills the functional and non-functional requirements of the customer and its users.

Firmitas (solidity):
The software is stable in terms of the specified quality requirements (for example, the number of simultaneously supported users). It also has to allow future enhancements without having to completely rebuild the system.

Venustas (elegance):
The software's structure makes it intuitive to use, but also easy to maintain and develop.

1.2   iSAQB: The International Software Architecture Qualification Board

Software architecture is an extremely young discipline and, despite many publications on the subject, various opinions still exist regarding its precise scope and design in the context of computer science and information technology. The tasks and responsibilities of software architects are defined in very different ways and are subject to continual renegotiation during a project.

In contrast, software engineering disciplines such as project management, requirements engineering, and testing have a more mature knowledge base. Various independent organizations offer training curricula that clearly define the knowledge and skills required by these disciplines (for testing, visit *www.istqb.org*; for requirements engineering, visit *www.ireb.org*; for project management, visit *www.pmi.org*).

In 2008, a group of software architecture experts from business, industry, and scientific communities formed the *International Software Architecture Qualification Board* as a registered association under German law (iSAQB e.V., *www.isaqb.org*). The goal of the iSAQB is to define product- and manufacturer-independent standards for the training and certification of software architects. Certifications at *Foundation*, *Advanced*, and *Expert* levels allow software architects to certify their knowledge, experience, and skills using a recognized procedure (see figure 1-3).

Because it eliminates the terminological uncertainty referred to earlier, standardized training benefits established and aspiring software architects, companies, and training organizations. Precise training curricula are essential for the examination and certification of aspiring software, and ensure that high-quality training is available on the basis of an accepted canon of knowledge.

Certification as a *Certified Professional for Software Architecture* (CPSA) is carried out by independent bodies. CPSA *Foundation Level* certification is based on a subset of a non-public catalogue of demanding questions developed by the iSAQB and matched to the curriculum. *Advanced Level* certification also requires practical certification and participation in licensed training courses (or acknowledgement of equivalent non-iSAQB qualifications). *Expert Level* certification is currently in development.

**Expert Level
(planned)**
The Expert Level addresses experienced,
professional software architects and consists of a series
of modules with different specialized topics. A Certified Professional
for Software Architecture Expert Level Block, which will requires
the foundation and advanced level certificate, is in the planning stage.

Advanced Level
The Advanced Level deepens the foundation level topics.
Developed according to iSAQB's specification, this training
scheme follows a modular structure and requires successful trainees
to demonstrate comprehensive knowledge and skills
(Examples: Architecture Documentation, SOA, Soft Skills for Software Architects).

Foundation Level
Training to become an iSAQB Certified Professional for Software Architecture comprises all knowledge
areas a specialist for software architecture is required to know. The training modules deal with tasks, methodologies,
techniques and technologies for the development of software architectures. Participants get to know all aspects that
are essential for software architectures. In addition to technological factors, organizational and social factors get addressed.
Thus, the tasks of a specialist for software architecture are broadly covered.

Figure 1-3   *iSAQB certification levels (www.isaqb.org)*

Various licensed training institutions offer multi-day courses designed to refresh and deepen candidates' existing knowledge in these subject areas. Participation in a course is recommended, but is not a prerequisite for registration for the certification examination.

1.3   Certified Professional for Software Architecture – Foundation and Advanced Level

The iSAQB has now defined clear certification guidelines for CPSA *Foundation Level* and *Advanced Level* certification.

Advanced Level certification is modular and consists of individual courses dedicated to specific core competences for IT professionals:

- **Methodical competence**
  Technology-independent skills for systematic approaches to IT projects

- **Technical competence**
  Skills in the use of technology for solving design tasks

- **Communicative competence**
  Communication, presentation, rhetorical, and meeting skills that increase efficiency during the software development process

Prerequisites for *Advanced Level* certification are:

- CPSA-F (*Foundation Level*) training and certification
- At least 3 years' professional experience in the IT sector
- Active participation in the design and development of at least two different IT systems
- At least 70 credit points from all three competence areas (with a minimum of 10 credit points for each)

The examination consists of solving a prescribed task and discussion of the solution with two independent examiners.

For *Foundation Level* certification is based on knowledge and skills defined in the iSAQB curriculum [isaqb-curriculum]. These are as follows:

- The definition and importance of software architecture
- The tasks and responsibilities of software architects
- The role of the software architect within a project
- State-of-the-art methods and techniques for the development of software architectures

The focus is on the acquisition of the following skills:

- Coordinating critical software architecture decisions with other parties involved in requirements management, project management, testing, and development
- Documenting and communicating software architectures on the basis of views, architectural patterns, and technical concepts
- Understanding the main steps involved in the design of software architectures and performing them independently for small and medium-sized systems

Foundation Level training provides the knowledge necessary for designing and documenting a solution-based software architecture for small and medium-sized systems, based on a sufficiently detailed requirements specification. This architecture can then serve as a template for implementation. Participants are trained to make problem-oriented design decisions on the basis of previous practical experience.

Figure 1-4 shows the content and weighting of the individual areas of the curriculum for iSAQB *Certified Professional for Software Architecture (CPSA) Foundation Level* training.

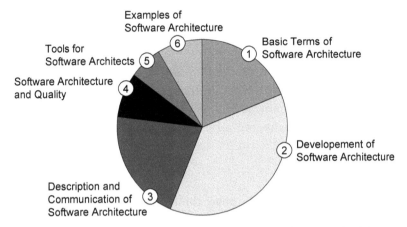

Figure 1-4   *Structure of the iSAQB curriculum for the CPSA Foundation Level training*

Various independent bodies offer certification based on the iSAQB curriculum. Examiners use standardized questions prepared by the iSAQB.

Questions are multiple-choice, so the results are objectively measurable.

The examination validates your software architecture capabilities on paper. It is up to you to prove yourself in real-world situations.

1.4   The aim of this book

Members of the iSAQB developed this book during the creation of the *Certified Professional for Software Architecture, Foundation Level* curriculum. The main aim of the book is to provide a concise summary of the knowledge required to pass the CPSA *Foundation Level* examination, and thus the basic knowledge required for the creation of successful software architectures. This makes the book an ideal reference manual when preparing for the examination. In addition to reading the book, we also strongly recommend participation in the corresponding training courses, which offer practical examples of software architectures and the personal experience of our training staff, both of which go beyond the scope of this book.

The book focuses primarily on methodical skills and knowledge, so specific implementation technologies and tools are not part of the standardized training content. Specific notations and acronyms (such as UML) are to be understood only as examples. The book does not describe individual, specific procedure models or specific development processes, and instead provides various examples.

It explains important terms and concepts involved in software architecture and their relationships with other disciplines. Building on this, it provides an introduction to the fundamental methods and techniques required for design and development, description and communication, and quality assurance in software architectures. It also addresses the roles, tasks, interactions, and work environment of software architects, and describes how they integrate with company and project structures.

1.5   Prerequisites

In line with the aims described above, the book and the iSAQB curriculum assume you have previous experience in software development. The following content is neither part of the book nor the curriculum, although it forms an essential part of every software architect's skill set:

- Several years of practical experience in software development, gained by programming differing projects or systems
- Advanced knowledge of and practical experience with at least one high-level programming language
- Fundamentals of modeling, abstraction, and UML; in particular class, package, component, and sequence diagrams and how they relate to source code
- Practical experience in technical documentation; in particular the documentation of source code, system designs, and technical concepts

Knowledge and experience of object orientation is also advantageous for an understanding of some of the concepts involved. Experience in the design and implementation of distributed applications (such as client-server systems or web applications) is also desirable.

1.6   Reader's guide

The structure of this book is primarily oriented to the structure and content of the iSAQB *Foundation Level* curriculum. For more details, see figure 1-4 and [isaqb-curriculum]:

- In Chapter 2 we describe terms and software architecture basics, which are then addressed in more detail in subsequent chapters. For example, the concept of a software system "view" is introduced within the context of software architecture.

Practical software architecture design is addressed in Chapter 3. Topics covered include variants of the architecture development procedure; important architectural patterns such as views, pipes and filters, and model view controllers; and design principles such as coupling, cohesion, and separation of concerns.

Chapter 4 covers proven description tools and guidelines that enable you to document your software architecture and communicate it to others. This is oriented toward a specific target group. Topics covered include the iSAQB view model and cross-cutting concerns in software architectures.

In Chapter 5 we take a look at the relationship between software architecture and quality issues. Important terms include quality, quality characteristics, ATAM (Architecture Tradeoff Analysis Method), quality tree, compromises (in the implementation of quality characteristics), qualitative architecture evaluation, and the risks involved in achieving quality assurance objectives.

Chapter 6 lists sample support tools for modeling, generating, and documenting software architectures.

The appendices include sample questions, a glossary, and a list of reference resources.

Chapters 2 to 5 are essential when preparing for the iSAQB examination, and the other sections are useful too. For general reading, we recommend that you thoroughly read Chapter 2 and then move on to the topics that interest you most.

1.7   Target audience

The primary target audience for this book is anyone who is preparing for iSAQB certification and/or attending iSAQB training courses. The book is also aimed at IT professionals and students who wish to familiarize themselves with the basic terms used in software architecture.

The book also provides an overview of software architecture for software project managers, product managers, and decision makers at the intermediate software development level.

1.8   Acknowledgements

We would like to take this opportunity to thank the iSAQB for its support, and in particular our iSAQB reviewers of previous editions Andreas Rothmann, Phillip Ghadir, and Stefan Zörner. Many thanks to Roger E. Rhoades for the review of the English text. We would also like to thank Ingrid Schindler from the Chair for Software Systems Engineering at Clausthal University of Technology, and the staff at ITech Progress, who provided invaluable support in the preparation of the diagrams. In particular, Christine O'Brien and Robert Kerns have been very supportive in creating the English edition of this book, thank you!

Our thanks also go to our editor Christa Preisendanz for her patience.

Finally, we particularly want to thank our families and partners who gave us the time and space to work together on this book.

2   Software Architecture Fundamentals

As already explained in the introduction, software is nowadays just about everywhere. For almost a full 24 hours a day we rely on software operating correctly, starting with the alarm clock in the morning, via proper functioning of car and train brakes, through to the management of our money in bank accounts.

Despite this omnipresence and our dependence on software, we software engineers have still not understood in sufficient detail how to successfully construct software on a repeatable basis. Software projects take too long, cost too much, and fail too often. And even when a software project successfully goes into operational use, the result is often inadequate for those involved. This is confirmed time and time again on an annual basis in the CHAOS Report from the Standish Group [Sta99]. Despite all the criticism of the CHAOS Report, the fact can not be denied that other methods for evaluating success provide very similar, less than flattering results (see [EK08], [EV10]). The bottom line is that our ability to successfully manage software projects within the magic rectangle (see [Bal00], [Die00], [Dum01], [Lit05], [May05]), as shown in figure 2-1, is extremely limited. We are still not able to create high-quality software repeatably with the necessary functionality at affordable costs and within the specified timeframe.

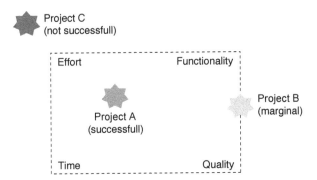

Figure 2-1   *The magic rectangle of successful software projects*

Two key factors for successfully developing software are requirements engineering and architecture design. With both of these disciplines the risk of serious undesirable developments is high, since decisions with far-reaching impacts (that in some cases can only be identified much later in the course of the project) have to be made at an early stage—in particular when the level of available knowledge is still limited (see [Nus01], [GEM04]).

For this reason, software architecture is one of the decisive success factors in software development, since it decides how to structure millions of lines of program code for large, software-intensive systems in such a way that the specified functionality is available in the end result with the desired quality, within budget, and on time (see fig. 2-1).

So what does software architecture actually involve? What are the central concepts in this decisive sub-discipline of software engineering? What procedures and approaches are available for successful architecture design?

Software architecture, like software engineering, is a young discipline. There are therefore many different opinions on the above issues, and we do not wish to decry these in any way or disqualify them as incorrect. In this chapter we instead wish to explain our fundamental understanding of software architecture, and thus provide the basis for the chapters that follow.

First we will present the term "software-intensive system" and its relevance to software architecture. Building on this, we then present and define the central fundamental terms of software architecture. Finally, we will introduce the fundamental procedures involved in architecture design and explain the interactions with other disciplines and roles.

2.1   Integration with the iSAQB curriculum

An extract from the *Fundamental terms used in the context of software architectures* section of the iSAQB curriculum [isaqb-curriculum] is provided below.

2.1.1   Learning goals

LG 1-1:   Discuss definitions of software architecture

LG 1-2:   Understand and identify the benefits and objectives of software architecture

LG 1-3:   Understand software architecture as part of the software life-cycle

LG 1-4:   Understand software architects' tasks and responsibilities

LG 1-5:   Relate the role of software architects to other stakeholders

LG 1-6:   Ability to explain the correlation between development approaches and software architecture

LG 1-7:   Differentiate between architecture and project objectives

LG 1-8:   Distinguish between explicit statements and implicit assumptions

LG 1-9:   Know roles and responsibilities of software architects in an organizational context

LG 1-10: Understand the differences between types of IT systems

2.2   Software-intensive systems and software architectures

Software architecture always manifests itself in the associated system, irrespective of whether it was explicitly designed or has simply evolved. We must therefore first develop a clear understanding of what a software-intensive system really is, before we can take a more detailed look at the architecture of such systems. In the following sections we will therefore first define the term "software-intensive system" and discuss different types of software-intensive systems. Building on this, we can then establish the relationship to the software architecture of the addressed systems.

2.2.1 What is a software-intensive system?

First of all there's a fundamental question here: What is a system? We can find an answer to this question in IEEE Standard 610.12-1990, the *IEEE Standard Glossary of Software Engineering Terminology*. A system is defined there as follows:

> **System.** A collection of components organized to accomplish a specific function or set of functions.
>
> [IEEE 610.12-1990, p. 73]

That definition—which appears quite intuitive—appropriately characterizes the essential attributes of a system. A system consists of building blocks and components such as hardware, software or mechanical building blocks.

This definition of a system also includes the concept that systems can be broken down into building blocks. In accordance with the definition above, a system must also serve a specific purpose. This reflects the fundamental understanding of engineering, namely to create things with a beneficial impact on the quality of people's lives (see the NSPE Code of Ethics for Engineers [NSPE]).

The second essential element of a "software-intensive system" is the term "software". In this case too, we find a definition in the IEEE Standard Glossary of Software Engineering Terminology:

> **Software.** Computer programs, procedures, and possibly associated documentation and data pertaining to the operation of a computer system.
> [IEEE 610.12-1990, p. 66]

Software is accordingly more than just a collection of program files. Software also includes additional procedures such as configuration scripts, associated documentation (e.g. an architectural description), and data (e.g. the initial filling of a database with the necessary metadata and master data).

In order to formulate a definition of a software-intensive system in the context of this chapter, we need to combine the two definitions above and also include the intensive role of the software in the system. Based on this approach, a software-intensive system is defined as follows:

> A **software-intensive system** is a collection of building blocks that are organized in such a way that they together accomplish the purpose of the system. Building blocks of such a system that entirely or for the most part consist of software carry out essential tasks for achievement of the purpose of the system. The software element of the system consists of a collection of programs, procedures, data, and associated documentation.

2.2.2 Types of software-intensive systems

Different approaches exist for categorizing software. Each of these approaches places emphasis on specific attributes, and is consequently not universally applicable. In its definition of the term "software", the *IEEE Standard Glossary of Software Engineering Terminology*, for example, differentiates between application software, support software and system software:

Software. ... See also: application software; support software; system software.
[IEEE 610.12-1990, p. 66]

This differentiation depends on the context in which the categorization takes place. The database of an insurance system is, from the customers' point of view, system software. From the programmer's point of view, however, it is support software. Or consider a web browser: From the point of view of a computer user who wants to surf on the Internet, the web browser is application software. From the viewpoint of the programmer whose task is to create a plug-in for it, the web browser is system software.

Another frequently encountered differentiation is the one between standard software and custom software [Sie04]. These and other attempts to categorize software (for example, on the basis of size or application domain) ultimately result in a multidimensional classification as shown in figure 2-2. The classification here is not always distinct, and in most cases depends on the viewer's perception, as noted in the previous paragraph.

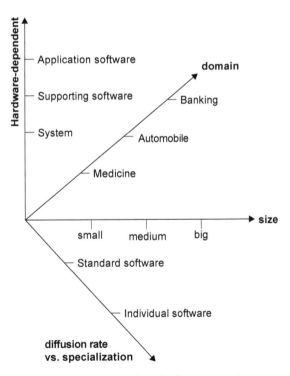

Figure 2-2   *Multi-dimensional categorization of software-intensive systems*

Categorization of software is helpful to us, since it permits initial inferences to be made about the software architecture. In an ideal world, a series of architecture approaches and architecture-specific design problems could be predefined for each category of software. This predefinition would then reflect the collective design experience of the software architects. Software architects would then have an easy and reliable start to their design task.

Unfortunately neither a standardized categorization system for software nor a related and complete collection of design know-how exists. It is also not clear whether it will ever be possible to build up and use such a knowledge base in an environment as dynamic as the software industry. For this reason, each individual software architect and software organization has to compile and expand this for themselves.

The fundamental approach and the goal are nonetheless worth following. For this reason, in this chapter we want to carry out a simple categorization and also, by way of an example, at least partially establish a link to software architecture. Figure 2-3 shows a possible classification into the following categories:

The focus of **information systems** is on management and processing of information. Large amounts of data or complex data structures have to be managed, processed, evaluated and calculated, and several thousand users may have to be served both simultaneously and interactively. Examples of information systems are the core insurance management system of an insurance company, SAP systems, CAD systems, complex simulation systems for weather forecasting, or simulation calculations for engineers.

Embedded systems contain software that is embedded into physical objects. With significant resource limitations in terms of the available hardware, they carry out tasks that are critical in terms of both data security and functional reliability, and which have to fulfill demanding functional and quality requirements. This functionality mostly involves regulation, control or communication functions. Examples of embedded systems are washing machines, machine tools or production lines in the manufacturing industry, radio cells in mobile phone networks, airbag control systems, and vehicle parking assistants.

Mobile systems are (semi-)autonomous, personal units with high interaction requirements. In addition to being mobile, they are characterized by the fact that they provide local and, where necessary, (semi-)autonomous functions. In addition they can, and to an extent also need to, interact with centralized, mainly stationary systems to synchronize themselves or to coordinate information and actions with others. Due to their mobility, however, the link to the central systems is not continuously available. Examples of embedded systems are smartphones, (semi-)autonomous transportation robots, and sensor/actuator nodes in ad-hoc networks.

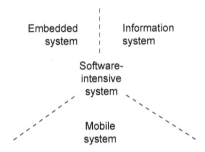

Figure 2-3   *Categories of software-intensive systems*

With the increasing networking of systems, software-intensive systems exist that cannot be assigned to merely one category. An insurance system, for example, integrates an insurance broker directly into the system via an app on a smartphone. Via an Internet connection and a web browser, SAP evaluation reports can be analyzed directly in vehicles. Additionally, almost all of a factory's production lines are nowadays already connected via the associated manufacturing execution system to the factory's SAP system, and vice versa.

Despite the fact that many of today's systems cannot be unambiguously assigned to one of the three categories defined above, each system nonetheless has its key focus. In cases of doubt, it is clear to all involved whether the system in question or the design task to be addressed should be categorized as an information system or an embedded system.

This is particularly important for software architects, since for each of these categories there are specific basic patterns and approaches in terms of software architecture and architecture design. With information systems, for example, one usually finds a layered architecture, whereas embedded systems involve architecture with active processes or modules that are loosely coupled but nonetheless interact with each other via networks (for example, via bus-based communication). With mobile systems one also has an architecture with active processes, but in this case the processes mainly communicate using shared memory, since they run on a single (possibly multicore) processor.

For each category there is also a specific set of architecture-relevant design problems, particularly with regard to specific, non-functional requirements. With information systems, for example, one has to consider the nature of data management and the associated transaction control. With embedded systems on the other hand, the scheduling of the active processes or the communication load on the network is more relevant. And with the mobile devices, it's more a case of striking a balance between the required high-quality but resource-intensive graphical user interface and the sensor and actuator-specific functions at the hardware level.

2.2.3   The importance of software architecture for a software-intensive system

As already explained in the introduction, designing software architecture is an important and critical step in software development. The software architecture has a direct impact on the parameters of the magic rectangle depicted in figure 2-1. These are the desired functionality, the associated quality characteristics, the effort necessary for creating the system, and the time required until the system can be deployed. Ultimately, the question is how to structure large systems so that the desired parameters of the magic rectangle can be achieved.

But does every software-intensive system actually have its own software architecture? In the same way as structures that came into being without the involvement of a building architect, each software-intensive system has an architecture, even if it wasn't explicitly designed and implemented. In development projects one can, regrettably, too often see cases where the software architecture has not been explicitly designed. The consequences are often serious.

Software requirements change during the course of development, and also during the software's entire lifecycle, regardless of how well they are documented. Changing requirements impact the development project. For example, project plans have to be changed or the budget adjusted. All of this is futile, however, if the already implemented software elements are incompatible with the desired changes. Good software architecture, however, makes it easy to change existing functionalities or introduce new functionalities without endangering the quality characteristics of the existing software.

Software architecture is thus of enormous importance for successful software development. What, however, is the reason for this? We will briefly address this question using two sub-questions: Why does all software have an architecture? Why is the software architecture a decisive factor for successful software development?

An essential element of good software architecture is the mainly hierarchical decomposition of the system into subsystems or building blocks. The existence of such a decomposed structure is also already part of the nature of software-intensive systems. As already mentioned in the definition above, a software-intensive system consists of a collection of building blocks that are organized so that they accomplish the purpose of the system. The birth of the architecture is thus inextricably linked to the definition of a system. Each (software-intensive) system thus has an implicit or explicit architecture.

This inherent dovetailing concept—that the software architecture decisively defines the system structure and vice versa—is also the reason why software architecture is a decisive factor for successful software development. The structure of buildings defines which components are crucial load-bearing elements and which are not. If you want to change part of a building without affecting its load-bearing elements, that is usually possible without any problems. If, however, load-bearing elements have to be modified, then it's difficult to predict whether and how that can be achieved and how much it will cost.

This also applies analogously to software architecture, which defines the critical elements in the software via the definition of the system structure. The software architecture thus defines the framework for future changes. Should requests for change or new features arise during the course of the development project or the subsequent lifecycle of the software, these can be fulfilled without problems as long as the critical cornerstones of the software are retained. Otherwise the same applies as for buildings—in other words, costs, time, and the resulting quality are extremely difficult to estimate, and the relationship between costs and benefits is normally not acceptable.

This banal but fundamental relationship between the software-intensive system, the inherently existent software architecture, and the resulting limitations to the magic rectangle is the reason for the enormous significance and implications of software architecture in software development.

2.3 Fundamental software architecture concepts

Software architecture defines the essential structures, overall technical concepts, and design decisions of a software system, and is the basis for the development of the entire system. It can thus be regarded as a construction plan that sustainably eases the development of complex and extensive software. The software architecture does not specify the detailed design, but instead describes a constructive path to a solution, starting from the requirements placed on the system from the outside, through to the fully constructed system that results—for example, in the form of program files. During this process, the reasons for the design decisions should be documented wherever possible, since the selection of a specific architecture has a significant influence on the quality attributes as well as non-functional characteristics such as maintainability, extendibility, and performance.

Despite its importance, software architecture is still a young discipline. For this reason, this chapter provides a general introduction to the fundamental concepts of software architectures. First we define our understanding of the term "software architecture" based on the terms "building block" and "interface", which will also be introduced. This provides us with the basis for describing what software architectures are good for and what benefits they can generate. This is then rounded out with concepts for describing software architectures.

2.3.1 What is a software architecture?

There is no single, universally accepted definition of software architecture. As an introduction to the many definitions of software architecture, here is a fairly exotic but nevertheless appropriate definition:

> Software architecture is a framework for change.
>
> (Andreas Rausch, see also [SEI Def])

The Software Engineering Institute at Carnegie Mellon University (SEI) has collected more than 150 definitions of software architecture on a website specially created for this purpose [SEI Def]. A consensus, which we endorse, can increasingly be identified among the formulated definitions. It is also reflected in the definition provided by IEEE Standard 42010:2011, *Recommended Practice for Architectural Description for Software-Intensive Systems*:

> <system> fundamental concepts or properties of a system in its environment embodied in its elements, relationships, and in the principles of its design and evolution.
>
> [ISO/IEC/IEEE 42010:2011]

Rather than introducing a completely new definition for this central term within the scope of this chapter, we orient ourselves to this standard but supplement it in a few places, for example using the term "interface" and a reference to the development organization, since we regard these as fundamentally important for software architectures.

> The **software architecture** defines the fundamental principles and rules for the organization of a system and its structure into building blocks and interfaces, and their relationships to each other and to the surrounding environment. It thus defines guidelines for the entire software lifecycle, the developer, and the software's operator, from analysis via design and implementation to operation and enhancement.

This understanding of software architecture includes two significant aspects. Firstly the constructive aspect, which specifies the structure of a software-intensive system and its division into building blocks and interfaces, and their relationships to each other and the surrounding environment. The definition, however, also includes a second aspect with regard to procedures. Software architecture also influences the developer and the system lifecycle, and thus specifies which principles and rules have to be observed.

This also means that software architecture objectives can also be long-term objectives that extend beyond project objectives and their time horizon, which is usually coupled to the duration of the development project. Software architecture can thus also represent and include an investment in the entire system lifecycle, which possibly only amortizes itself following completion of the associated development project.

2.3.2 Building blocks, interfaces, and configurations

We will now take a look at the system construction aspect of software architecture. The terms "building block" and "interface" and the relationship between these elements will be introduced.

"Interface" and "building block" are fundamental engineering terms. They are also popular in information technology, but although they are used almost on a daily basis, there is no common, precise understanding of what an interface or a building block is.

The fact that interfaces and building blocks are not understood in the same way by everyone can be seen when, for example, electrical engineers, mechanical engineers, and computer scientists are simultaneously involved in a system development project. If you try to reach agreement with all parties involved on an interface for the machine tool to be developed, you will soon discover that completely different concepts exist regarding what an interface is and what it isn't. So at this stage we wish to define the term "interface" as follows:

> An **interface** represents a well-defined access point to the system or its building blocks. In this context, an interface describes the characteristics, (for example, attributes, data, and functions) of this access point. The objective is to define these characteristics as precisely as possible with all the necessary aspects, such as syntax, data structures, functional behavior, error behavior, non-functional characteristics, the interface usage log, technologies, protocols, access modifiers, file formats, conditions/constraints, and semantics.

This definition of an interface clearly shows that the comprehensive specification of interfaces can be extremely laborious. Programming languages such as Java or C# contain interface concepts with which one can normally define the syntax, (the name of the interface), the methods provided, and their arguments and return values. Other aspects of an interface—for example, its functional behavior—have to be recorded in additional documentation.

We often find only inadequate interface descriptions in the programs. If, for example, you look at the *Collection* interface in Java, it appears to be extremely well prepared and documented. On the other hand, there are no statements in regarding the performance of the *Insert* operation for inserting an element into a Collection (for example, the upper and lower limit, or the average time allowed for the insertion of an element).

For the use of this interface, however, this characteristic can be highly relevant, particularly in the case of processor-intensive tasks on a large number of elements. These characteristics are critical when it comes to deciding whether the Java *Collection* should be used, or an alternative solution has to be found.

In this special case, the programmer therefore has to be aware of the specific implementations of the interface and select the appropriate one. In this case he can choose either the *ArrayList* or the *LinkedList*, which have different performance characteristics. The interface thus doesn't completely encapsulate the implementation, despite the fact that this is its defined task.

This example illustrates that it is generally not possible to create complete interface descriptions. It is more often left to the architect to decide which aspects of an interface have to be described and which can be neglected in cases of doubt. You should nonetheless attempt to create complete interface descriptions wherever possible, with relevant characteristics for the specific project context.

We can now address the term "building block". The term "building block" is often used as a synonym for "component". However, while "building block", is a general term, "components" are a special form of building blocks. In this respect we have consciously decided against the term "component" since it is often understood to mean something else. Some people understand components to primarily mean UML components, while others associate components with programming constructs such as packages or JavaBeans.

We use the colloquial term "building block" to abstract component elements of a software architecture from the multitude of terms used in programming languages, modeling approaches, and design methods. A building block in our context is thus an abstraction of special programming constructs or descriptive elements.

The building block is the central basic element from which the static structure of a software architecture is constructed. It includes all software or implementation artifacts that ultimately represent abstractions of source code. This ranges from small building blocks (such as functions or classes) via medium-sized building blocks (such as packages or libraries) through to large building blocks (such as subsystems, layers or frameworks). Building blocks can thus manifest themselves in different ways. Figure 2-4 shows some examples of specific types of building blocks. It should be noted here that building blocks can themselves consist of other building blocks.

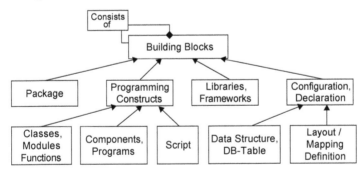

Figure 2-4   *Examples of building blocks*

The term "building block" is thus one of the most important terms in software architecture. It requires clear criteria, however, for the purposes of delimitation. What is a building block and what is not? Our definition of a building block includes the three essential characteristics specified below, and thus extensively subsumes the dominant definitions found in relevant literature ([Szy 98], [D'SW98], [RQ+12]).

A **building block** provides interfaces that it guarantees in the sense of a contract. This guarantee, however, only applies when the interfaces that it requires are made available within the scope of a corresponding configuration. (**Provided and required interfaces**)

Via the provided and required interfaces, the building block encapsulates the implementation of these interfaces. It can thus be replaced by other building blocks that provide and, where appropriate, also require the same interfaces. (**Encapsulation and interchangeability**)

Building blocks are also the unit of hierarchical (de)composition of a software-intensive system. In other words, a building block can be implemented using an appropriate configuration of other (sub-)building blocks and their interrelationships. In this case, too, we say that this (super) building block encapsulates the (sub-) blocks. The building block can also delegate external interfaces to internal interfaces and vice versa. This is how relationships between building blocks are defined. (**Configuration and hierarchical (de)composition**)

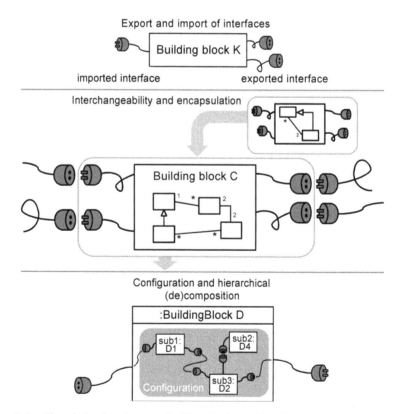

Figure 2-5   *The relationships between building blocks and interfaces*

Please note: Due to possible side effects, the required interfaces must also be taken into account when replacing building blocks. A building block is a reusable component. Further assumptions—for example, regarding the surrounding environment of the building blocks and the existence of the interfaces required by a building block—should be kept to a minimum and be explicitly documented.

The term "building block" has now been explained, and the possible relationships between building blocks and interfaces have been defined. The essential characteristics of building blocks have also been determined as follows: Provided and required interfaces, encapsulation and interchangeability, configuration and hierarchical (de)composition. Figure 2-5 illustrates these terms and their interrelationships.

As shown in figure 2-6, we can differentiate between different views of a building block:

In the **black box view** we only see the interfaces provided and required by the building block. This is the view seen by the user of the building block. This view respects the information-hiding principle—in other words, it hides the (private) internal details of the building block. The black box view can, for example, be described using UML component diagrams.

The **gray box view** shows which additional, mostly technical interfaces are required by the building block—for example, configuration interfaces or interfaces to the runtime environment that are required and used [BW97]. The gray box view can be described using UML distribution diagrams.

The **white box view** (also known as the glass box view) provides a view of the internal details of the building block—in other words, its decomposition into the configuration of the sub-building blocks or a different type of implementation. This view also shows the delegation of its provided and required interfaces to the internal workings of the building block. This is the view seen by the implementer of the building block. The white box view can, for example, be described using UML composite structure diagrams.

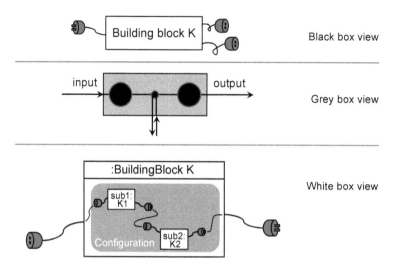

Figure 2-6   *Black box, gray box, and white box views*

The hierarchical (de)composition of an architecture and its buildings blocks becomes particularly clear in the interaction between black box, gray box, and white box. As shown in figure 2-7, the black box view of a building block A can be hierarchically decomposed in the white box view below it. In this white box view, building block A is broken down into the component elements B1, B2 and B3.

Please note: The elements b1, b2 and b3 are not building blocks, but placeholders (also referred to as "parts" in UML) that use an instance of a building block. We also refer to these placeholders as building block instances, or simply building blocks if there is no important difference. For the sub-building block instances b1 to b3 there are also placeholders for building block instances in the configuration of building block A. Not all building block instances, however, can be used by the placeholders b1, b2 and b3, since the placeholders have specific types. Placeholders are comparable to variables in that they have a value (= building block instance) and a type (=building block). The placeholder "b1 : Building block B1" can thus only use an instance of building block B1.

Since this building block instance defines the building block type in the configuration, there is also a black box view for this building block.

It should be noted here that the diagram only shows one hierarchy in the context of the description of the architecture. Instances of a building block can thus be used in multiple configurations of other building blocks, viewable in their white box views. Building blocks may also be used at different hierarchical levels. In figure 2-7, building block B1 appears as a building block instance in the configuration of the white box view, both as a sub-building block instance of A and as a sub-building block instance of B2. B1 could be an XML parser building block that is used in a wide range of different building blocks at a number of different levels.

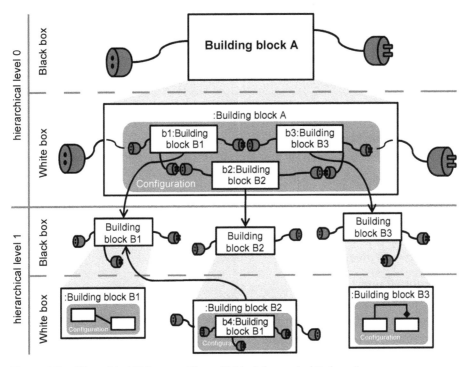

Figure 2-7   *Hierarchical (de)composition with black box and white box views*

It should also be noted that this hierarchical decomposition applies not only to the building blocks, but also to their interfaces. In other words, if a building block has an interface to another building block in the gray box, a corresponding interface also exists at the black box and white box levels, and must naturally be implemented accordingly—for example, by delegating the interface to a sub-building block.

Interfaces are used to connect building blocks. Both building blocks must comply with the interface agreement, regardless of whether they provide or require the interface. This is defined in the interface itself. But who defines the interface? There are different possibilities here:

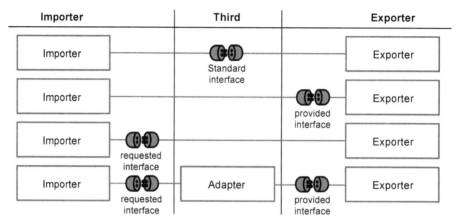

Figure 2-8   *Who defines the interface and the interface agreement?*

Standard interface
This interface is defined by an external third party. Both the providing and requesting building blocks comply with it.

Provided interface
In this case the interface is defined by the building block that provided it. Apart from the standard interface, this is the type of interface that is most commonly used.

Required interface
In this case the interface is defined by the building block that requires it. This configuration is often found within frameworks. With these types of interfaces you can incorporate building blocks with specific functionality into a program structure.

Independent interfaces
In this case both the building block that provides the interface and the building block that requires it define their own interfaces. This increases the decoupling of the building blocks, and they can be developed and tested independently. This, however, means that the interfaces do not remain identical over the course of time, and for this reason an adapter has to be placed between them.

Each interface definition type has its specific characteristics, and thus also advantages and disadvantages. The final variant of the interface definition type increases the decoupling of the building blocks, but has to be paid for with increased development effort and extended timescale. This variant can nonetheless be considered a reasonable long-term solution—for example, in the case of integration tasks.

On the other hand, this variant can also be used on a temporary basis to ensure maximum concurrency during development while uniting inconsistent developments. In this case, however, you need to budget additional time for refactoring and redesign of the architecture to enable removal of the adapter, with new common interface agreements. Otherwise, the temporary solution will unintentionally become a permanent solution.

2.3.3   Concepts for describing software architectures

Regardless of whether it has evolved explicitly or implicitly, an architecture is only of limited use if it is not documented. Only an appropriately documented architecture can be sustainably communicated, discussed, and further developed.

Software architecture is not only discussed with other architects. All aspects of the software architecture are presented to representatives of different interests (stakeholders), discussed with them, and jointly further developed. Customers and users, for example, can also become involved in architecture decisions that affect them. Developers should also become involved in the discussion, in particular for communication and discussion of aspects of the architecture that are relevant to the final implementation.

In accordance with IEEE Standard 42010:2011, Recommended *Practice for Architectural Description for Software-Intensive Systems* [IEEE 42010:2011], a software architecture description contains a collection of artifacts for depicting a software architecture. The corresponding standard defines a conceptual model for architectural descriptions. Figure 2-9 shows the part of the conceptual model that is of particular interest to us.

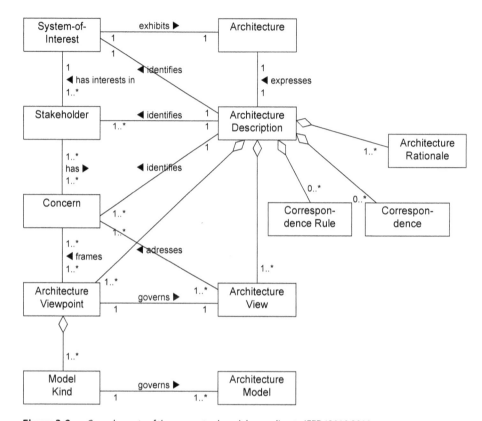

Figure 2-9   *Core elements of the conceptual model according to IEEE 42010:2011*

In this excerpt from the model, a system is influenced by its environment and vice versa. Each system has an architecture. In accordance with the IEEE standard, this architecture is described by a single architectural description. At first glance this would appear to be a limitation. However, as explained above, the standard defines an architectural description as consisting of a collection of artifacts. This means that an architecture is documented by a collection of descriptions. This could (and should) be stated more clearly in the standard.

A system also has a number of stakeholders, and stakeholders in turn have a number of concerns. The architectural description addresses the stakeholders' concerns and uses them to justify the architecture decisions made in the associated rationales.

In this respect, the standard covers a widespread core concept of many software architecture approaches, namely: that architectural descriptions include views of the architecture. The concept of views is illustrated in figure 2-10. A stakeholder has a different view of the architecture depending on his viewpoint. These viewpoints are motivated by each stakeholder's own particular concerns.

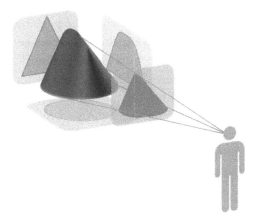

Figure 2-10   *Views are projections of the software architecture.*

The IEEE standard describes multiple "views", including a "functional view", a "physical view", and a "technical view", which are often referred to as separate architectures or architectural levels—for example, as "functional architecture" or "functional levels".

Architecture Viewpoint
An architecture viewpoint is a set of conventions for constructing, interpreting, using and analyzing one type of architecture view. A viewpoint includes model kinds, viewpoint languages and notations, modeling methods and analytical techniques to frame a specific set of concerns. Examples of viewpoints are: operational, systems, technical, logical, deployment, process, information.

Architecture View
An architecture view in an AD[1] expresses the architecture of the system of interest from the perspective of one or more stakeholders to address specific concerns, using the conventions established by its viewpoint. An architecture view consists of one or more architecture models.

[ISO/IEC/IEEE 42010]

---

1 AD = Architecture Description

In other architecture approaches—for example, the 4+1 architecture model from Kruchten [Kru95], the views are motivated by the different descriptive elements in different diagrams. In Kruchten's logical view, for example, the focus is on building blocks and their relationships, while the process view describes processes and the exchange of information between them.

In addition, relevant literature frequently refers to many different architectures or architecture levels. These include business process architectures, IT architectures, functional architecture levels, technical architectures, technical infrastructure architectures, deployment architecture levels, and many other terms (see for example [EH+08], [Sie03]).

A refreshingly original differentiation in this terminological muddle is provided by Siedersleben's "Blood Groups" [SD00]. Take an application architecture layer (Blood Group A) and a technical architecture layer (Blood Group T). As with blood groups, mixing of the architecture layers is undesirable. Another type of differentiation can be found in the Zachmann Framework [O'RF+03], where architecture levels are differentiated in two dimensions according to roles and perspectives.

In summary, it can be stated that the terms architectures, architecture layers, and views are used all too frequently to describe architectures. Against this background, we define a simple conceptual model (see figure 2-11) for the description of software architectures.

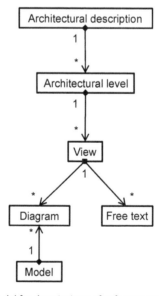

Figure 2-11   *Conceptual model for descriptions of software architectures*

In accordance with this definition, an architectural description consists of a collection of architectural levels. An architectural level combines a number of views to form a meaningful descriptive element. Views include both text and diagrams, which in turn are stored in models.

A functional architecture level can, for example, contain both a static view consisting of a collection of static diagrams (see the building block view in Section 4.3.5), and a dynamic view consisting of a collection of behavior diagrams (see the runtime view in Section 4.3.6). Additional free-text descriptions, however, are essential for documenting and understanding the architecture. Furthermore, the rationales already referred to for the architecture decisions form a part of this text. Some levels consist solely of free text.

2.3.4 Architectural description and architectural levels

As already explained, an architecture is described at different levels. The selection and organization of these levels provides an initial reference point for the associated design methodology. Architectural levels are often found at different levels of abstraction—for example, a high-level "service-oriented layered architecture" style, or a more specific functional architectural level that includes functional entities and services.

There are a large number of different approaches and standards for architecture methods and their associated description methods. Some of these—such as TOGAF®, RM-ODP, and the Zachman Framework—are introduced in Chapter 4. One fundamental principle however, shown in figure 2-12, is common to all of these methods. The methodology in all of these architecture approaches is based on a separation of the associated description and refinement approach into two dimensions. In the perspective dimension, different architectural areas (such as data, processes, services, and program organization) are addressed. In the degree-of-abstraction dimension, these different architectural areas are addressed and described step by step in increasing detail. Once you have understood this approach, it will be relatively easily to navigate your way around each of these architecture frameworks.

As an example, figure 2-12 shows a subdivision of the architectural description into four architectural levels: the architectural style, technical infrastructure, the functional application architecture level (also referred to as A-architecture), and the technical architecture level (T-architecture). As shown below, these four levels differ in two dimensions—in other words, in terms of both the level of abstraction and perspective (functional vs. technical).

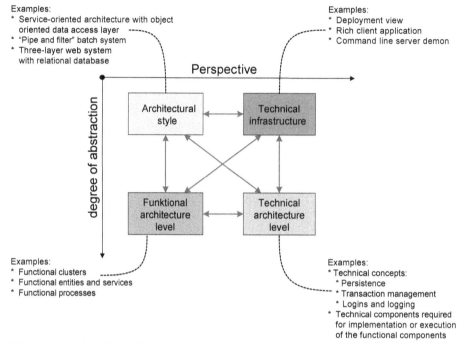

Examples:
* Service-oriented architecture with object oriented data access layer
* "Pipe and filter" batch system
* Three-layer web system with relational database

Examples:
* Deployment view
* Rich client application
* Command line server demon

Examples:
* Functional clusters
* Functional entities and services
* Functional processes

Examples:
* Technical concepts:
  * Persistence
  * Transaction management
  * Logins and logging
* Technical components required for implementation or execution of the functional components

Figure 2-12   *The different levels in an architectural description*

As the arrows between the levels illustrate, the architectural levels can be addressed individually, although they mutually influence each other and are thus interdependent. The more specific functional and technical architectural levels naturally involve the requirements of the architectural style and the technical infrastructure. In the one direction, the specific designs of the functional and technical architectural levels influence the requirements on higher architectural levels. Analogous relationships can be found in the other dimension. For example, technical architecture provides specific concepts for persistence or transaction management, which in turn have to be included at the functional architectural level. In the other direction, the functional architectural level provides the inputs in terms of the required persistence concepts.

The architectural style here is the central architectural metaphor of the system. For example: "Our software system is structured as a three-layer architecture using a model view controller in the presentation layer and object-relational mapping in the data management layer." On the other hand, the technical infrastructure defines the network profiles of the architecture. For example: "We have a thin client with a web and application container and a relational database."

The view-based description of the functional and technical architectural levels takes place at the more detailed architectural levels (see also [SD00]). At the functional architectural level, appropriate application building blocks and their relationships are designed for the implementation of the functional requirements. For example, a design can be created here for a generic insurance product model that enables mapping of different insurance products in the application.

In contrast, at the technical architectural level cross-disciplinary solution building blocks are designed and documented for the relevant aspects based on non-functional requirements. For example, versioning of all functional entities may be necessary, and a solution for this is developed in the technical architecture. The functional entities on the application architecture level can then use this general solution from the technical architectural level.

2.3.5   Interactions between software architecture and environment

As figure 2-12 shows, the architecture of a system is not created in a vacuum, but is influenced by the surrounding environment and vice versa. The elements surrounding the actual software architecture are frequently also referred to as architectures—for example, a business process architecture. We wish to avoid the use of the term architecture here to avoid overloading it. Instead, we increasingly use the terms "environment" or "landscape". Figure 2-13 shows the essential surrounding areas within the context of software architecture and the roles involved in them:

Project environment and project management
Project environment and project management provide a variety of constraints and project objectives that must be taken into account where they are relevant to the architecture. Budgets and the development approach, for example, can influence the software architecture, and vice versa. In the surrounding environment of a system there are usually a number of applications and projects. This existing (and continuously changing) project and application landscape often has significant impacts on the software architecture being developed. If additional projects or applications are initiated or suddenly terminated, this can have enormous impact on interfaces to the system for which a software architecture is to be developed.

Product Management and Requirements Engineering
Product Management and Requirements Engineering place functional and, in particular, non-functional requirements, quality objectives, and

constraints on the system, all of which can change during the course of the project and thus affect the architecture. On the other hand, the architecture can also identify which requirements generate conflicts of interest with other requirements or project constraints. The architecture can thus also generate impulses for changes to requirements.

Execution platform and operation

Generally, the execution platform and operations organization already exist within the organization. New systems should use existing systems where possible, and this should be taken into account during the architecture design. On the other hand, new platform and operations requirements can also result from the architecture.

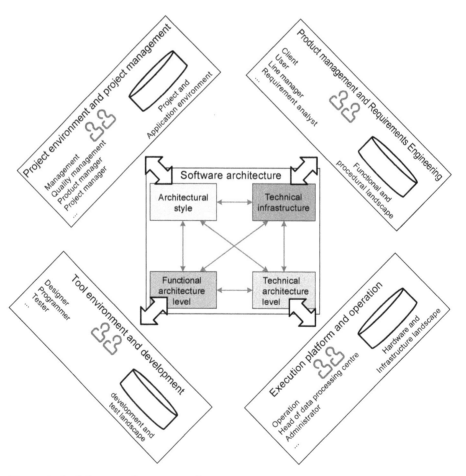

Figure 2-13 *Software architecture is influenced by its environment and vice versa.*

Tools and development environment

The architecture must ultimately be implemented. This requires appropriate tools and a development organization. Appropriate development environments also have to be provided for the selected programming languages, frameworks, and technologies. Equally, the architecture itself can also place new requirements on tools and the development organization. Expansion of the test infrastructure may, for example, be necessary, depending on the selected technology.

2.3.6 Quality and value of a software architecture

But when is a developed or provided software architecture a good software architecture? [BCK03] defines a good architecture as one that enables a project and the system to fulfill their objectives within the context of the magic rectangle (i.e., costs, time, functionality, and quality), while factoring in the lifecycle. As with all quality attributes, the quality of an architecture is subjective and depends on who is assessing it [ISO/IEC 25010].

In other words, a software architecture is only suitable for the specified objectives, constraints, requirements, and future challenges to a certain extent. The externally perceived quality of a software architecture can only be evaluated in the context of specific quality objectives. The required quality characteristics are derived from the current and future objectives, constraints, and requirements, and are thus specific to the individual software system in question.

However, current and future objectives, constraints, and functional requirements (and in particular non-functional requirements) are often not described sufficiently and completely. In this respect, it is worth taking a look at ISO Standard 25010 [ISO/IEC 25010], in which high-level quality characteristics are already defined:

- Functional Suitability
- Reliability
- Usability
- Performance efficiency
- Security
- Maintainability
- Compatibility
- Portability

These quality attributes are good starting points for deriving additional quality characteristics for the software architecture and the software system. In addition, the existing objectives, constraints, and requirements and the required quality characteristics derived from them can also be checked for completeness using the FURPS attributes (see also Section 2.4 and Chapter 5).

In addition to explicitly formulated objectives, constraints, and requirements, from which the required quality characteristics are derived, each project also has a variety of implicit objectives, constraints, and requirements. During checking of the completeness of the required quality characteristics, these implicit (and still hidden) quality characteristics must—where possible—be made completely explicit. For example, there may be an implicit condition that a specific database management system is to be used, since it is the standard system in the company, licenses have already been paid for, and the operation of the database is ensured. Non-explicit constraints with regard to time-to-market can also result in implicit architectural requirements in terms of incremental approach support. These implicit objectives, constraints, and requirements must be made explicit, and the quality characteristics that have to be implemented must be derived from them. This is the only way to ensure that they are taken into account and implemented in the designed architecture.

In addition to externally perceptible quality, quality not seen directly by the user also plays a role. In the product design of modern vehicles, for example, components are designed and installed to simplify future recycling of precious metals or rare earth. These quality characteristics are not obvious to the owner, but may be manifested indirectly in the vehicle's price.

Quality objectives that are not immediately perceptible to the user are also inherently defined with the software architecture, independent of the specific software-intensive system. If the software architecture is defined as a central value during system development, a range of quality objectives implicitly results. For example, the software architecture must be easy to understand, transparent, have up-to-date documentation, and be implemented correctly. Ease of development and a structured project organization must be supported by the architecture. It should also ensure simple and economic system operation, extensibility, and maintainability. The greatest possible reuse of existing building blocks is desirable for both quality-related and economic reasons.

2.4   A bird's-eye view of software architecture design

As already explained in the introduction, requirements engineering and architecture design are two key factors for successful software development. The risk of unwanted developments is particularly high in these areas, which is why they also offer the greatest potential for risk minimization and general optimization.

It is not sufficient to address these two areas in isolation. On the contrary, it is essential to ensure consistent integration of requirements engineering and architecture design if they are to influence each other positively. The so-called Twin Peaks Model (cf. [Nus01]) emphasizes this relationship, and requires iterative collaboration of requirements engineering and architecture design, as shown in figure 2-14.

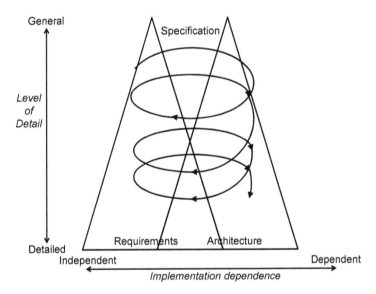

Figure 2-14   *The Twin Peaks Model [Nus01]*

The impacts of requirements in terms of the effort involved can only be realistically assessed when an initial high-level architecture design is available. If the efforts assessed on the basis of the high-level architecture design are then presented to the customer, it is not uncommon for them to waive certain requirements. However, existing design alternatives can indicate to those responsible for specifying the requirements that the requirements are not sufficiently precisely defined (see also [HM+07]).

2.4.1   Objectives and functions of software architecture design

The central task of software architecture design is to find a design approach with which the functional and non-functional requirements defined by requirements engineering are implemented in a fully designed solution. This approach, however, is not a one-way street, as indicated by the Twin Peaks Model shown in figure 2-14.

Instead, the process involves continual compromise between the "request list" from requirements engineering and the software architect's inventory of existing solutions, building blocks, and other architecture artifacts. As figure 2-15 illustrates, this approach means the software architect develops the construction plan for the software system in coordination with relevant stakeholders (such as the requirements engineer, the customer, the user, the developer, the tester, or the administrator).

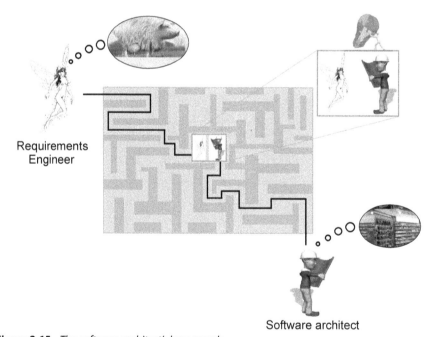

Figure 2-15   *The software architect's long march*

Since a new system or system enhancements should not be addressed in isolation, interfaces to other systems, affected organizations, execution platforms, and the implementation infrastructure also have to be taken into account. The interfaces, requirements, and constraints from the four adjacent areas (see fig. 2-13) must be considered and co-designed by the architect.

The architect must also take the entire lifecycle of the system and the adjacent areas referred to above into account. Architecture always means investment in supporting elements in order to achieve flexibility and extensibility elsewhere. This, however, demands consideration of the corresponding lifecycles; otherwise, these investments may not be secure.

2.4.2   Overview of software architecture design

Software architecture is not developed behind closed doors, and demands teamwork from the many parties involved in the project. It is therefore necessary to develop a common understanding of what forms part of a software architecture and what does not, both within the current project and in its surrounding environment. This includes a common nomenclature for the most important terms such as "interface" or "building block".

As shown in figure 2-13, the architect not only has to consider interfaces with requirements engineering, but also with other disciplines and roles involved in software development. A software architect designs an architecture starting from the conditions, constraints, and requirements of these surrounding areas, thus defining the essential aspects of the solution, such as the building block structure and interaction patterns. Viewed in isolation, the architecture design process is not sequential. Even the term "iterative approach" doesn't sufficiently describe the nature of the architecture design process. The individual tasks involved in the process cannot be meaningfully brought into a linear sequence. Instead, as shown in figure 2-16, we subdivide architecture design into four activities of equal weighting:

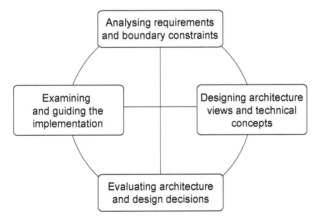

Figure 2-16   *Iterative and incremental steps involved in software architecture design*

Analysis of requirements and constraints

The central task of architecture analysis is to analyze the objectives, constraints, and the functional (and in particular, non-functional requirements) that come from requirements engineering in the context of the other surrounding areas (cf. figure 2-13). This must include an analysis of quality, flexibility (the stakeholder is open to changes), and susceptibility to change (changes as a result of external influences over time) of the requirements. Gaps in the requirements must be identified (see [HNS99]). Particularly with regard to non-functional requirements, there is normally room for improvement since those responsible for specifying the requirements often regard them as being self-evident. All parties involved in the project—especially designers and developers—have to develop an initial understanding of the architecture style and the technical infrastructure. This is the central architectural metaphor of the system.

Development of architecture views and technical concepts

Here, the architecture is developed in more detail. In particular the view-based description of the different architectural levels (functional and technical levels—see figure 2-13) also takes place here. The objective is to break down the functional requirements to the corresponding functional architecture level, and for the relevant aspects of the non-functional requirements to design and document appropriate cross-cutting solution building blocks at the technical architecture level (see also Chapter 4). All the while, the fundamental solution framework given by the architecture style and the technical infrastructure must be taken into account.

Evaluation of architecture and design decisions

The developed architecture must undergo quality assurance. Various methods can be used here, from diverse review techniques through technical prototypes and tests to analysis and evaluation. The critical aspect here is the derivation of specific scenarios from the requirements to ensure the quality of the resulting architecture (see also Chapter 5).

Implementation support and review

The importance of the communication of software architecture to all parties involved in the project is often underestimated. Only when all those involved—from the developer through to the customer—have understood and accepted the software architecture, can it be successfully implemented and achieve the desired effects. The software architecture must of course be communicated in such a way that it can be understood by the recipient.

This means that the architecture is explained to the customer with a different level of detail than to the developer. This process is not a one-way street, but rather a process of learning from one another and understanding. During its implementation, the architecture continues to be discussed with the parties involved in the project and any open issues, potential for improvement, faults and errors, and approaches for further development continue to be identified.

Effective tool support should also be established on the basis of these concepts. This ensures optimal support for the individual areas of activity involved in the design of the software architecture—for example, analysis and management of requirements, handling of architecture models and documentation, quality assurance, and communication. Autonomous tool solutions already exist for these individual task areas (see Chapter 6). These stand-alone tools must be integrated as seamlessly as possible to ensure that the architect can use them effectively. Because the design process is not sequential but rather iterative and incremental (or even concurrent), it is especially important to close the gaps between the individual tools.

2.4.3   Interplay between activities and abstraction levels within the design

As already explained, the individual activities involved in the software architecture design process cannot be arranged linearly. They are areas of equal importance to which the software architect has to devote sufficient attention depending on the current project situation. The architecture design is a continuous interplay between the activities shown in figure 2-16:

- Analysis of requirements and constraints
- Development of architecture views and technical concepts
- Evaluation of architecture and design decisions
- Support and review of the implementation

During the architecture design process, the software architect carries out these four activities in a sequence that suits the needs and context of the project. This iterative and incremental interplay of activities is associated with a top-down and bottom-up change of the abstraction levels and perspectives shown in figure 2-13:

Requirements and constraints of the surrounding areas
Software architecture with abstraction levels, for example:

Architecture style and technical infrastructure
Functional and technical architecture levels

Program design and implementation

This way, we can switch from the topmost abstraction level of the conditions, constraints, and requirements of the surrounding areas via the abstraction levels in the software architecture (architecture style and technical infrastructure, plus the functional and technical architecture levels) through to the bottommost abstraction level, which consist of the software program itself, the program's design and its implementation. The architecture design process is thus a continuous top-down and bottom-up flow within the abstraction levels along with a continuous change of activities that are performed interactively and incrementally. This is illustrated in figure 2-17.

Within this process, the project setting and constraints define the constraints of the architecture. In return, the architecture design provides data on technical project risks and planning information.

Requirements engineering describes the functional and non-functional requirements for the architecture design coming from those accountable for the system. As explained above, this is not a one-way street, and the architecture design also provides feedback on the feasibility of implementing the requirements, and their consequences for requirements engineering.

The partially or fully available technical infrastructure—for example, server infrastructure, operating systems, requirements for programming languages, and the operating organization—must also be taken into consideration during the architecture design process. Especially the interface with operations is far too often neglected, which can result in major problems during system deployment. And once again, this is not a one-way street. The architecture design can produce new technical infrastructure requirements—for example, further expansion of the server landscape or the integration of additional middleware.

Finally, the architecture design provides the specifications for detailed design and programming. However, return flows of information are also necessary here. Unforeseen problems can arise during the implementation of the software architecture and, if these are not communicated to the software architect and a supposedly simple solution is implemented instead, this can undermine the entire architecture. It is therefore important to discuss such problems with the software architect, and to jointly develop a solution that may result in changes to the architecture.

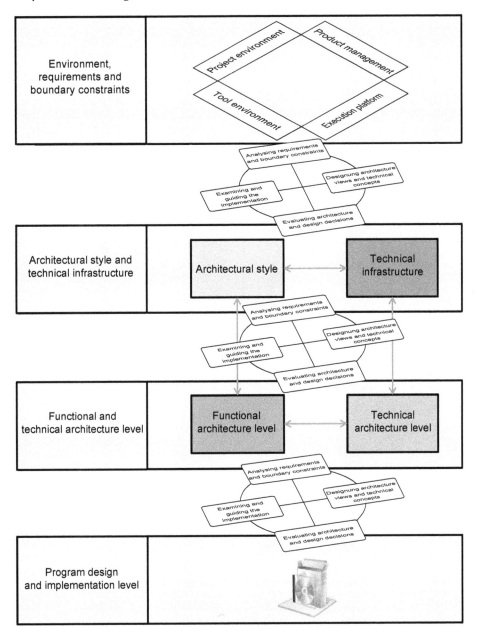

Figure 2-17 *Overview of the software architecture design process*

2.4.4　A software architect's tasks and relationships with other roles

The task of the architect is to develop a blueprint for the system based on the functional and non-functional requirements, while taking requirements and constraints of the surrounding areas into account. The subsequent implementation, maintenance, support and enhancements are then based on this blueprint. This requires development of a complete and concise architectural description. The architectural description serves on the one hand as a communication and discussion platform, and on the other hand as a design and implementation plan. As shown in figure 2-18, the architect must provide a large number of interfaces to almost all of the roles involved in a software development project.

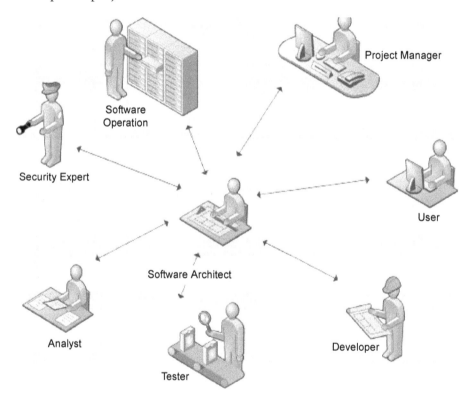

Figure 2-18　*The software architect in relation to the neighboring roles*

Communication and discussion platform
Based on the architecture, the architect presents the feasibility of the requirements to the requirements engineer, the customer, and possibly the

user too. During this process, the architect provides support by correlating, prioritizing, and reflecting on functional and non-functional requirements. He can identify contradictions and discrepancies, and ultimately ensures that the requirements can be implemented. The architect identifies ways of integrating existing solutions and systems, and aligns the requirements to the existing system architecture and hardware. He develops, evaluates, and assesses alternative solution approaches. Finally, based on the software architecture, the architect advises the project manager on project and iteration planning, and supports risk analysis and mitigation, thus providing support for the definition of work structure and assignment.

Design and implementation plan
The architect is a central point of contact for the system's developers. He defines the system's building blocks as well as their interfaces and interaction patterns. He has to encourage the integration of new technologies and innovative solution approaches, and discuss them with the developers. He is in charge of the development, introduction, training, and reviewing of programming guidelines. He assists the developers in the development of prototypes and sample solutions, and accelerates reuse of existing (partial) implementations. He explains the architecture, provides development specifications, passes on his experience, and carries out code reviews. He also supports the testers. In an ideal situation, he even defines testing conditions and specific test cases for testing specific architecture objectives. He assists in the definition of test sequences and dependencies. Finally, he is the point of contact for fault and error reports that are relevant to the architecture. He is also the central point of contact for organizational roles such as operations staff, security experts, and the like.

2.5   Test your knowledge

Here are some detailed excerpts from the *Fundamental terms used in the context of software architectures* section of the iSAQB curriculum [isaqb-curriculum] to help you consolidate what you have learned.

LG 1-1: Discuss definitions of software architecture

  Comparison of several definitions of software architecture and identification of their similarities

  Understanding the terms and definitions of software architecture

Software architecture is not the solution, but rather the design and description of the solution.

LG 1-2: Understand and identify the benefits and objectives of software architecture

Software architecture focuses more on quality attributes such as durability, maintainability, changeability, and robustness than on pure functionality.

Software architecture supports the creation, maintenance, and implementation of software.

Software architecture supports the fulfillment of quality requirements.

Software architecture supports understanding of the system for all relevant stakeholders.

LG 1-3: Understand software architecture as part of the software lifecycle

Understanding the correlation with business and operational processes for information systems

Understanding the correlation with business and operational processes for decision support systems (data warehouse, management information systems)

Understanding that changes of requirements, quality goals, technologies, or in the system's environment might require changes to the software architecture

LG 1-4: Understand a software architect's tasks and responsibilities

Software architects are responsible for achieving the required or necessary quality and functionality of a solution. Depending on the approach or process model used, they must align this responsibility with the overall responsibilities for project management and/or other roles.

Software architects clarify and question requirements and constraints, and refine them if necessary. Together with functional requirements (required features), this includes the required quality attributes (required constraints).

Software architects decide how to decompose the system into building blocks, while determining dependencies and interfaces between the building blocks.

Software architects determine and decide cross-cutting technical concerns (such persistence, communication, GUI, and so on).

Software architects communicate and document software architecture based on views, architectural patterns, and technical concepts.

Software architects accompany the realization and implementation of the architecture; if necessary, they integrate feedback from relevant stakeholders into the architecture; they review and ensure the consistency of source code and software architecture.

Software architects evaluate software architecture, especially with respect to risks involving the required quality characteristics.

It is the responsibility of software architects to identify and highlight the consequences of architectural decisions and discuss these with other stakeholders. Their role involves recognizing the necessity of iterations in all tasks, and pointing out opportunities for providing relevant feedback.

LG 1-5: Relate the role of software architects to other stakeholders

Software architects are able to explain their role. They should adapt their contribution to software development in a specific context and in relation to other stakeholders, in particular to:

- Requirements analysis (system analysis, requirements management, specialist field)
- Implementation
- Project lead and management
- Product management/product owner
- Quality assurance
- IT operations (production, data centers). This applies primarily to information systems.
- Hardware development

LG 1-6: Ability to explain the correlation between development approaches and software architecture

Software architects are able to explain the influence of iterative approaches on architectural decisions (especially with regard to risks and predictability).

Due to inherent uncertainty, software architects often have to work and decide iteratively. To do so, they must systematically seek feedback from other stakeholders.

LG 1-7:   Differentiate between architecture and project objectives

Systems can be developed within projects, scrum sprints, iterations, releases, or other approaches. The term "project" above refers to any of these approaches to the organization of work.

Software architects should be able to demonstrate the significance of architectural objectives, constraints, and influencing factors for the design of software architectures.

They can explain the connection between requirements and solutions.

They can identify and specify architectural objectives based upon existing requirements.

They can explain (long-term) architectural objectives and the distinction between these and (short-term) project objectives.

LG 1-8:   Distinguish between explicit statements and implicit assumptions

Software architects should explicitly present assumptions or prerequisites and avoid implicit assumptions. They know that implicit assumptions can lead to misunderstandings between stakeholders.

LG 1-9:   Know roles and responsibilities of software architects in an organizational context

Software architects know about additional architecture levels, such as Infrastructure architecture, hardware architecture, software architecture, enterprise IT architecture, and business process architecture.

LG 1-10: Understanding the differences between types of IT systems

Software architects can differentiate software architecture requirements and approaches for different types of IT systems.

3 Designing Software Architectures

In the previous chapter we presented the fundamentals of software architectures, and explained that the software architecture defines a design approach for the implementation of the functional and non-functional requirements defined by requirements engineering in a fully designed software system. Finding the right design approach or, in other words, the design of the software architecture, is what this chapter is all about.

As with the creation of a new algorithm for a complex, not completely formulated problem, architecture design is a creative process. The creation of a software architecture is much more than the work of an individual architect working alone, meditating until divine inspiration provides him with the right solution. This approach is doomed to failure, particularly in the case of complex software systems. You cannot expect an uncoordinated design to be accepted and implemented without contradictions by all the parties involved in the project. It is equally unrealistic to expect that a single person can keep track of all requirements and the consequences of his decisions. Communication between all involved parties is a significant success factor that must be taken into account during the design process.

In the first section, we provide an overview of the architecture design process. This is followed by proven design principles and heuristics, such as top-down and bottom-up, "divide and conquer", and the simple-as-possible principle. In the sections that follow, we present a series of architecture-oriented development approaches that create links with existing and widely used methods and processes. We then address a series of techniques which, when appropriately applied, sustainably increase the quality of the design. Finally, we cover architectural and design patterns that offer a wealth of great ideas and solution building blocks for every architect.

3.1   Integration with the iSAQB curriculum

An extract from the *Designing software architectures* section of the iSAQB curriculum [isaqb-curriculum] is provided below.

3.1.1   Learning goals

LG 2-1: Select and adhere to approaches and heuristics for architecture development

LG 2-2: Design architectures

LG 2-3: Identify and consider factors influencing software architecture

LG 2-4: Decide on and design cross-cutting concepts

LG 2-5: Describe, explain and appropriately use important architectural patterns and architectural styles

LG 2-6: Explain and use design principles

LG 2-7: Plan dependencies between building blocks

LG 2-8: Design architecture building blocks/structural elements

LG 2-9: Design and define interfaces

3.2   Overview of the architecture design process

As already explained in Chapter 2, the architect moves in at least two dimensions during the design process (see fig. 3-1): on the one hand with top-down and bottom-up changes to the levels of abstraction and, on the other hand, in a continuous iterative and incremental interplay between the individual architecture design activities.

We differentiate between the following four levels of abstraction (see also Chapter 2):

Requirements and constraints
Software architecture levels of abstraction:

architecture style and technical infrastructure
functional and technical architecture levels

Program design and implementation

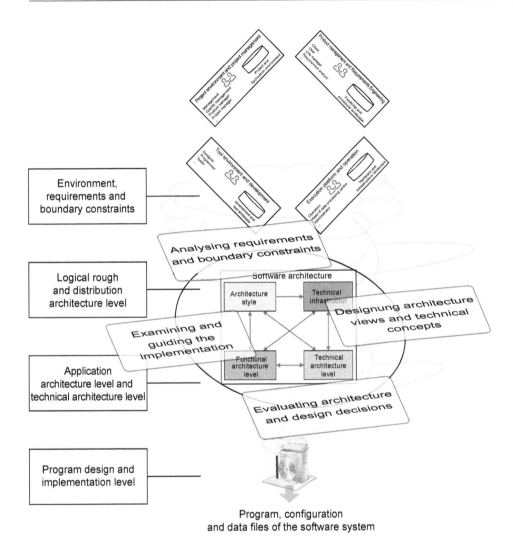

Environment, requirements and boundary constraints

Logical rough and distribution architecture level

Application architecture level and technical architecture level

Program design and implementation level

Program, configuration and data files of the software system

Figure 3-1 *Overview of the software architecture design process – iterative and incremental, top-down and bottom-up*

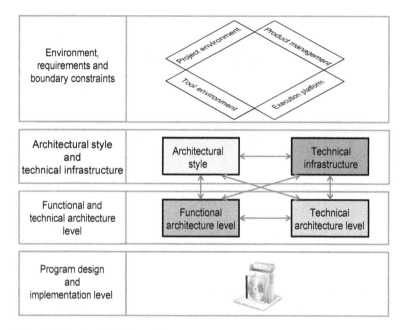

Figure 3-2   *The four levels of abstraction*

It should be noted here that a different number and structure of levels of abstraction is possible. In particular, other approaches such as model-driven architecture (MDA) contain more extensively differentiated levels of abstraction (see also Chapter 2 and Section 4.3). However, the levels of abstraction proposed here provide a general top-level structure and usually permit projection onto these types of approaches.

As shown in figure 3-2, changes between these levels of abstraction are made on both a top-down and bottom-up basis. During the design process the architect moves from the requirements and constraints abstraction level via the levels of abstraction in the software architecture down to the lowest abstraction level, which consists of the software program itself, the program design, and implementation.

The topmost abstraction level (requirements and constraints) is the input for the architecture design. The functional and non-functional requirements or architecture standards to be followed can be found at this abstraction level. The software architecture itself can be found on the two levels of abstraction below this.

At the architecture style and technical infrastructure level, a three-layer architecture with rich internet deployment is defined. At the application architecture and technical architecture level the design of the specific functional and technical components and their interaction takes place.

The final abstraction level (program design and implementation) is located at the implementation level. It thus represents the final goal of the software architecture designed above it—in other words, a developed software system. The software architecture also defines the corresponding architecture requirements and rules to be followed by the programmers.

The creative and inventive nature of architecture design means that the design process itself has to be iterative and incremental: iterative to incorporate feedback and new information, and incremental to continuously move development forward. This is why the individual activities involved cannot be meaningfully arranged in a linear sequence. They are all areas with equal weighting that the software architecture has to devote sufficient energy to depending on the specific project situation. There is no defined sequence for the four activities of the design process shown in figure 3-3:

- Analysis of the requirements and constraints
- Development of architecture views and technical concepts
- Evaluation of architecture and design decisions
- Support and review of the implementation

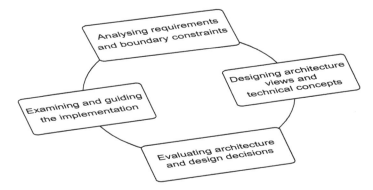

Figure 3-3   *The four major activities involved in the design process*

During the architecture design process the software architect carries out these four activities virtually simultaneously, but in a sequence appropriate for the context of the project and its needs. However, the sequence should adhere to the following fundamental principle:

During the first activity (analysis of requirements and constraints), the available input is normally analyzed from the next higher abstraction level, with the aim of creating central decision criteria for the design to be developed—for example, the criteria for the decomposition of the system into individual building blocks.

In the next activity (development of architecture views and technical concepts), the actual design work takes place. The design process essentially involves making decisions. Building blocks have to be identified for the solution, overall solutions then have to be developed for the addressed abstraction level, and the best possible solution has to be selected based on the decision criteria established during the initial analysis.

Next, the architecture and design decisions are evaluated. This is where previously defined requirements scenarios can be played out to test the architecture.

The final activity covers the support and review of the architecture implementation at the next lower abstraction level. An architect can of course actively support the implementation and is permitted to program too, if required.

The architecture design process is thus a continuous top-down and bottom-up flow within the levels of abstraction, associated with a continuous change of activities performed interactively and incrementally. The architect steadily and continuously moves in two dimensions (abstraction level and area of activity) during the design process. The moves within these dimensions are not chaotic, erratic steps, but rather deliberate actions on the part of the architect.

During this process the software architecture, the system, and overall organization influence and stimulate each other continuously. The iterative/incremental and top-down/bottom-up procedures assist in coping with uncertainties associated with the design, making it simpler to detect design issues at an early stage. It is therefore important to take central views, levels of abstraction, functionalities, and non-functional requirements into account as early as possible.

Due to the changes of abstraction level, the architect also comes into contact with different stakeholders. If he is in the requirements and constraints area, he will increasingly talk to the customer and the requirements engineer. At the program design and implementation level, the appropriate dialog partners are programmers and testers. One of the architect's tasks is thus to make full use of the central communication interface during the design process.

An architect who is currently in the "develop architecture views and technical concepts" activity area at the "architecture style and technical infrastructure" abstraction level may notice that two different deployment architectures are qualitatively equivalent, based on the previously derived decision criteria. Both a rich internet application and a fat client solution would equally well fulfill all the previously determined decision criteria.

The architect would then switch levels. At the "requirements and constraints" level, he would talk to the requirements analyst, explain the two alternatives to him and emphasize that requirements may be missing, thus determining which solution would be more favorable. The requirements analyst could discuss this with the stakeholders with the architect present. As a consequence, additional requirements could possibly be added to the requirements catalogue at this level.

The architect would then move back to the "analysis of requirements and constraints" activity area at the "architecture style and technical infrastructure" abstraction level, and would supplement the already created criteria catalogue with the aspects that result from the additional requirement(s). He would then take the extended criteria catalogue back to the "development of architecture views and technical concepts" activity area at the "architecture style and technical infrastructure" abstraction level, where he can now choose the better alternative based on the additional decision criterion.

Of course, this procedure doesn't take place as mechanically as presented here. It nonetheless reflects a typical, realistic sequence in the architecture design process. This sequence is accompanied by phone calls, discussions, and workshops. Even though it's not always transparent for the involved parties, the architect must always be aware of the level on which he is currently moving in two dimensions. This is the only way to ensure achievement of the right objectives, appropriate levels of communication, and an effective solution.

At the beginning of the design process, the first priority is to collect as much information as possible:

- Development of the domain knowledge and technical background knowledge necessary for the project
- Determination of existing systems in the organization and investigation of the extent to which they can be reused
- Determination of systems offered by third parties that perform a similar task to that of the system (or parts of the system) to be developed

  Reading appropriate technical literature in a search for the required solution approaches and procedural patterns

These are just a few examples of appropriate sources of information.

Based on this initial analysis, the central system concept can then be
defined. What is the central task? To this end, the main task and responsibility of the system should be described in a few sentences, with reference
to the most important terms and aspects of the functional domain. In most
cases, this already provides an initial framework for the architecture, since
this information enables us to assign the system to one of the three major
system categories: information system, mobile system, or embedded system
(see figure 2–3).

Depending on the system category, the next design steps and questions
are immediately clear. If the system to be designed is an information system,
a layered architecture would or might be used. Clarification is necessary on
whether an interactive system or a batch system is desired. Which business
processes need to be supported? Are transactions necessary using current
organization data? What availability and performance is required?

However, if we are talking about an embedded system, the questions to
ask are: Should it run on or control specialized hardware? Are there defined
time guarantee requirements for time-critical operations? Is result-based control necessary? Is there a need for parallel control?

These and other questions help the architect to prepare the following
steps. He must not, however, lose sight of the influencing factors and constraints, such as organizational and political aspects, technical and operational conditions/constraints, and the functional and non-functional requirements.

Organizational factors are things like the structure of the customer's
company, within the team, or of decision-making bodies. They can also be
related to the available resources—for example, personnel, budget, or schedule requirements. Organizational standards such as process models and tools
must also be taken into account. Legal aspects, too, need to be checked
and taken into account where appropriate. Technical and operational factors such as existing software and hardware infrastructure, programming
languages and styles, reference architectures, existing data structures, existing
libraries, and existing frameworks must not be neglected.

The architect must continuously address these and other influencing factors and constraints. In this respect, the topmost abstraction level (require-

ments and constraints) provides the corresponding reference points from the four areas:

- Project environment and project management
- Product management and requirements engineering
- Implementation environment and operations
- Tool environment and development

These interface areas are the sources of the requirements and constraints but also interact with the architecture. If the architect can convincingly argue that a change of requirements or constraints from these interface areas can simplify the architecture, the decision-makers will seriously consider taking appropriate action. The consequences for other architectures, systems, and organizations must then naturally be taken into account. This is how the functional and non-functional requirements are created for the architectural design, distilled by the requirements engineering department of the organization responsible for the requirements. The architecture design reflects the feasibility of the requirements and their consequences for requirements engineering. If we find that changes to a small number of requirements would significantly simplify the architecture, it is the task of the architect to discuss these options with the relevant interface roles and decision-makers.

3.3   Design principles and heuristics

Heuristics are methods and procedures used to solve problems with efficient use of resources.

Depending on the starting point and the problem to be solved, various methods and procedures addressed in this chapter can help—for example, top-down and bottom-up, "divide and conquer" or the separation of concerns.

In contrast to reference architectures that clearly demonstrate how a specific software architecture should be structured, architecture principles [VA++09] represent proven fundamental principles that nevertheless provide no information on how they are to be used in specific situations.

With most of the principles addressed here, two main issues play an important role. These are: reducing the complexity and increasing the flexibility (and adaptability) of the architecture.

3.3.1　Top-down and bottom-up

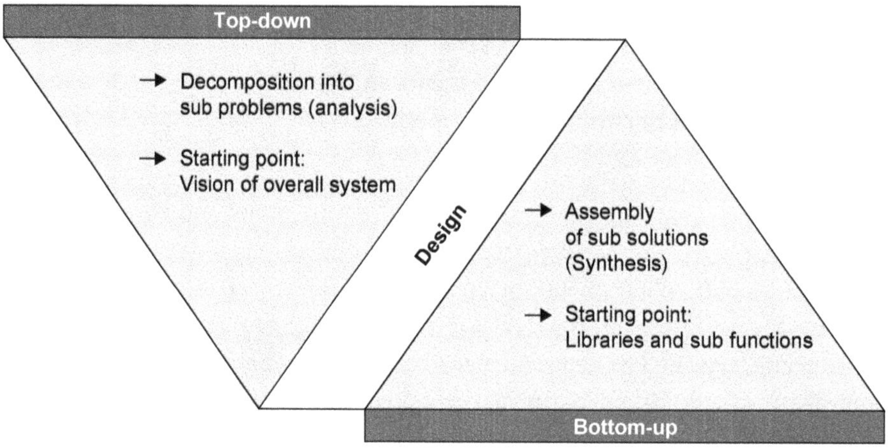

Figure 3-4　*Top-down and bottom-up*

The top-down approach starts with the problem, and successively breaks it down into smaller sub-problems, finally ending up with mini-problems that can no longer be broken down and that can be directly solved.

The advantages of this approach are that all components are known, and the risk of creating unsuitable results is extremely low. These advantages, however, are only visible at a late stage, and misunderstandings manifest themselves in the result at the end of the project.

Advantages	Disadvantages
Good understanding of the problem	Critical integration at the end
Machine and language-independent	Existing (partial) solutions may be overlooked
No risk of getting lost in detail	Significant changes necessary if problems are detected at a late stage
Clean interfaces consistency	Late feedback on whether the design does what it should
The design is visible in the product	

Table 3-1　*Top-down*

In contrast, the bottom-up approach starts with the specific machine and builds additional "abstract machines" on top of it. The developers start with the implementation without full knowledge of all system details. The partial solutions are combined with each other until finally a complete "problem solution machine" is created.

In contrast to the top-down method, results are achieved quickly, and risks are identified at an early stage. On the other hand, partial results can potentially be unsuitable for subsequent steps.

Advantages	Disadvantages
High degree of reusability	It is possible that not all parts will be required.
High functional reliability via incremental tests	Orientation to technical factors rather than user requirements
Incremental integration	Risk of premature optimization
Starts with assumed sub-problems	Risk of uncontrolled growth

Table 3-2   *Bottom-up*

The two approaches are not mutually exclusive and can complement each other.

3.3.2 Hierarchical (de)composition

3.3.2.1 Divide and conquer

The "divide and conquer" principle is used in many branches of IT and describes a reductionist approach that breaks a task down into ever smaller partial tasks until the complexity of these tasks reaches a manageable level. This principle is also used in numerous algorithms, and makes use of the fact that the effort required to solve problems is reduced when they are broken down into smaller sub-problems.

Similarities to the top-down design approach are clearly recognizable. A system or a component is broken down into ever smaller, relatively independent components, resulting in a hierarchical (or tree-type) component structure.

This approach can be used to encapsulate single or multiple functions or responsibilities, or to separate different aspects of a problem from one another.

Depending on the algorithm, various approaches are possible for solving the overall problem, for example:

The solution for the final sub-problem is also the solution for the overall problem. When searching in a binary tree, the final step of a search corresponds to the appropriate position in the tree.

Partial solutions are combined to form an overall solution.

The solution for the overall problem is selected in accordance with specific criteria from the best partial solution. With some optimization problems, the solution space is subdivided, and the optimal solution is sought among the partial solutions. From these optimal partial solutions, the best solution is then selected as the overall solution.

3.3.2.2 Decomposition principles

Decomposition is an important approach for reducing complexity [Sta11]. One of the central principles of decomposition is encapsulation, without which undesired dependencies between individual parts of the system can result. Encapsulate complexity in components and treat these as black boxes. Components should make no assumptions regarding the internal structure of other components.

Other important aspects are low coupling and high cohesion, but we will go into more detail on these later.

Instead of reinventing the wheel, you should reuse already established and proven structures.

Design iteratively, and determine and evaluate strengths and weaknesses based on a prototype design.

Break down the system into elements that are as independent as possible, and separate responsibilities clearly and understandably.

3.3.2.3 The "as-simple-as-possible" principle

As Albert Einstein once said, "Make things as simple as possible, but no simpler."

Simplicity has desirable effects. It makes things easier to understand and prevents problems becoming hidden by excessive complexity. Simple structures are easier to understand and are therefore easier to change. Any dependencies can also be more easily determined and more easily removed.

This principle is closely related to the term "suitability", as a degree of complexity can be appropriate in a specific situation. Appropriate use of complexity, however, is a matter of experience. In case of doubt, preference should be given to the less complex option.

3.3.2.4 Separation of concerns

The principle of separation of concerns states that different aspects of a problem should be separated from one another, and that each sub-problem should be addressed on its own. As with many other principles, it is based on the principle of "divide and conquer".

Concerns and responsibilities should be addressed at all levels of the design, from individual classes through to complete systems.

The separation of functional and technical elements is particularly important and should be a fundamental objective. Doing so ensures that the functional abstraction is separated from the specific technical implementation, and allows both aspects to be further developed independently of one another (or makes it easier to replace and reuse individual program elements). An additional advantage is increased quality due to improved traceability of changes and their impacts.

The modularity of a system determines the extent to which it is broken down and encapsulated in self-contained building blocks (modules). The principle of separation of concerns can be used in conjunction with the principle of information hiding to implement the modularity principle. The modularity principle states that one should aim to use self-contained system building blocks (modules) with simple and stable relationships. The building blocks of a modular system should be black boxes and hide their internal workings from the outside world.

3.3.3 Lean interfaces and information hiding

3.3.3.1 Information hiding

The principle of information hiding was developed by David Parnas in the early 1970s.

As already explained, the complexity of a system should be encapsulated in building blocks. This increases flexibility when it comes to making changes. The building blocks are regarded as black boxes; access to their internal structure is denied and instead takes place via defined interfaces. Only the subset of the total information that is absolutely necessary for the task should be disclosed.

3.3.3.2 Use of interfaces

The most important aspects of an architecture are interfaces and the relationships between building blocks. Interfaces form part of the basis of the overall system, and enable the relationships between the individual elements in the system. The individual building blocks and subsystems communicate and cooperate with each other via interfaces. Communication with the outside world also takes place via interfaces.

3.3.4   Regular refactoring and redesign

Putting the key into the lock and opening the door of a new house for the very first time is a wonderful experience. The individual rooms still smell of the final work carried out by the painters, carpenters, and others. Everything is clean, and the kitchen is tidy. A few weeks later the fresh smell has gone. And if you don't tidy up, maintain, repair, and throw things out on a regular basis, a new house can very quickly become an unattractive place.

The same principle applies to software and its architecture. Software is normally continuously enhanced. If you don't tidy up regularly and remove rough edges during the process, additional features created as a result of time pressure and bug fixing will not be integrated properly into the underlying architecture, and even the best software architecture will degenerate in a very short time. The costs for further development and renovation of software are often so high that the effort is no longer economically viable. Starting again from scratch then becomes an option that can't be excluded.

It is therefore necessary to "refactor" the software at regular intervals and to carry out a redesign. When defining "refactoring", Martin Fowler differentiates between the noun "refactoring" and the activity of "refactoring":

> Refactoring (noun) [Fow99]:
> "A change made to the internal structure of software to make it easier to understand and cheaper to modify without changing its observable behavior."

> Refactoring (verb) [Fow99]:
> "To restructure software by applying a series of refactorings without changing its observable behavior."

Refactoring serves to adapt dependencies so that incremental development is made simpler.

Take the example of a bugfix in a class that accesses another class via multiple dereferences in the format u.getV(). getW().getX().getY().getZ(). doSomething(). Such dereferencing chains should be avoided, since they create direct dependencies across entire networks of classes. In this case, a possible refactoring approach would be to place a new method getZ() in Class U.

It is critical that time is regularly spent on refactoring and redesign, and appropriate resources must be planned for in the overall project calculation.

3.4   Architecture-centric development approaches

In this section we present some contemporary architecture-centric development approaches and concepts used in the design and implementation of architectures. The goal is to provide a brief overview of development approaches that are architecture-centric. The list is by no means complete.

3.4.1   Domain-driven design

Domain-driven design (DDD) is a collection of principles and patterns that assist developers in the design of object systems. The term was coined by Eric Evans and, since it makes it easier to structure large systems by functional domains, is an important factor for developing a better understanding of microservices. Using this approach, each subsystem forms a separate unit.

3.4.1.1   Functional models as the basis for a design

You should begin your design by structuring the functional domain [Sta11]. The domain model should be structured on a purely functional basis and needs to be accepted throughout the project. This model improves communication between domain experts and developers, and enables precise formulation of requirements. The domain model can be tested extremely easily using direct mapping in the software. On the basis of this model, a common, domain-specific language is created whose elements should be included in the project glossary.

This universal language is the so-called *ubiquitous language*, and is a central concept of domain-driven design. This language should be used in all areas of software development—i.e., all project members should use the same terms as the domain experts in the source code as well as in databases and other components. It describes the functional domain, elements of the domain model, classes, methods, and so on.

Figure 3–5 shows the elements of a domain model created using domain-driven design.

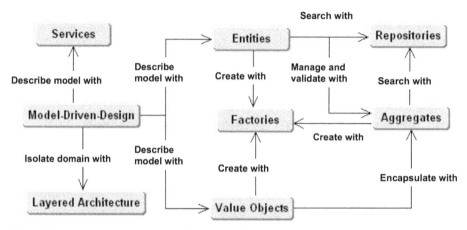

Figure 3-5   *Component elements of a domain model*

3.4.1.2 Systematic management of domain objects

The entities represent the core objects of a functional domain and are normally persistent. Within the domain they have a consistent identity and a clearly defined lifecycle. An entity is a "thing" in your system. It's often useful to imagine entities in the form of nouns (i.e., people or places).

Value objects describe the state of other objects and do not have an identity of their own. They simply describe objects that have identities. They can consist of other value objects, but never entities. In contrast to entities, value objects cannot be modified.

Services are operations that represent the process sequence of the domain. They are not recognized by entities and don't usually have a status of their own. The inputs and outputs of these operations are entities, aggregates, or value objects (i.e., domain objects).

For the management of domain objects, Evans recommends three different management objects:

Aggregates
An aggregate encapsulates interlinked domain objects and has precisely one entity in the form of a root object that represents sole access to the aggregate. External objects may only contain references to the root entity.

Factories

Factories encapsulate non-trivial, complex object structures. Factories have no access to other layers and serve exclusively for the construction of functional objects.

Repositories

A repository enables all types of objects to obtain object references for other objects, and encapsulates access by functional objects with the underlying persistence technology.

3.4.1.3 Structuring of the functional domain

The structuring of the functional domain normally takes place on the basis of functional objects or user transactions.

Decomposition based on functional objects is appropriate if

  Reuse is important.
  The functional logic is complex, extensive, or flexible.
  The object-oriented paradigm is well understood.

This type of decomposition more or less corresponds to object-oriented decomposition.

Structuring based on user transactions is appropriate in the case of

  Simple data acquisition and simple data operations
  Integration of external systems
  Simple or limited functional logic
  Limited experience with object-oriented procedures

A user transaction corresponds to an action that a system user can execute, including all system-internal operations such as checking input data.

The most important thing here is preservation of design integrity. Where possible, you should break down all parts of the system based on similar aspects and apply (and document) this concept consistently.

3.4.1.4 Types of domains

DDD subdivides a system into the following domains:

  Core domain
  Generic subdomain
  Supporting subdomain

The core domain contains the core functionality of the system and describes the reason for the existence of the system. Where possible, it should only be implemented by the most experienced developers.

The generic subdomain contains functionality of importance to the business but which does not form part of the core domain—for example, the generation of invoices or sending of letters. It can be bought in or outsourced.

The supporting subdomain contains supporting and subordinate functionality, and can also be handled by less experienced developers. It should, however, be strictly separated from the core domain—for example, using an anti-corruption layer.

3.4.1.5 Integration of domains

As already mentioned, each subsystem should form a separate unit. A further important term in DDD is "bounded context", which makes it easier to determine the appropriate granularity for microservices. Each model has a context, and a complex functional domain very probably consists of several bounded contexts.

Various possibilities exist for the integration of different domains. These include:

Published Language
There should be a common language via which the domains can interact—for example JSON or XML.

Open Host Service
This is a classic SOA form of interaction. One domain specifies a protocol via which other domains can use it—for example, the RESTful web service.

Anti-Corruption Layer
Uses services from another domain via an isolation layer.

Separate Ways
Two domains are completely separate from one another and have no integration.

3.4.2 MDA

Model-driven architecture (MDA) is a concept that enables the generation of (parts of) applications from models, such as UML. MDA was developed by the Object Management Group (OMG).

Model-driven software development (MDSD) generates software components automatically via transformations from models [RH06]. MDSD uses models and generators to improve software development.

The model forms the core of MDA, and is typically formulated with the aid of a domain-specific language (DSL). The DSL can either be text-based or graphical. However, a DSL is not mandatory. MDA, MDSD and other, similar approaches are DSL-independent.

There are two ways to create an executable application. Executable models are either interpreted directly by a virtual machine (such as the Object Management Group's *Executable UML*), or converted into an executable application by means of one or more transformations.

Model-driven architecture (MDA) as defined by the OMG is nothing more than a special instance of the MDSD approach, and has nothing to do with architecture. While model-driven software development offers a choice of modeling languages and no restrictions on transformation into executable applications, MDA has more specific requirements in this respect. For example, the DSL to be used should be MDA-compliant (i.e., defined using the OMG's Meta-Object Facility, or MOF, which forms the metamodel). In practice, mainly UML profiles are used.

The platform-independent aspects are modeled within the scope of a platform-independent model (PIM). The PIM is subsequently mapped to one or more platform-specific models (PSMs). The PSM thus creates the link to a specific platform, from which the code can then be generated.

The MDSD approach essentially has the following advantages:

- Increased development efficiency
- Specialist experts can be better integrated
- The software can be modified more easily
- Improved implementation of the software architecture
- The functional logic can be relatively easily ported to other platforms

Model-driven software development, however, requires establishment of an infrastructure consisting of DSLs, modeling tools, generators, platforms, and so on, as well as plenty of discipline when creating models. The specification effort is also greater, and usually only a part of the model can be automatically transformed into artifacts.

3.4.3   Reference architectures

3.4.3.1 Generative creation of system building blocks

If specific actions have to be carried out recurrently in the same or a similar way, they can be automated with the aid of generative techniques [VA++09]. Software systems often have to be created that differ only in a few details from other systems, with common features that are functional or technical. One overarching goal in software development is the greatest possible reuse of system building blocks.

Template-based generators are a popular means of software generation. A template in this context is mainly text-based. Part of the template accesses the input data, which are also largely text-based. Situations in which a template can be applied are defined with the help of patterns. Using predefined rules, the template is modified and the output is based on the generator input. Established examples of this approach are Java Emitter Templates (JET) or the XSLT transformation language, which forms part of the Extensible Stylesheet Language XSL and serves to transform XML documents.

Another generation technique uses API-based generators that are used (among other things) for generating PDF documents. In this case, the entire structure of the document to be generated is described via an API (Application Programming Interface).

Model-driven software development (MDSD) is a good example of the use of generators in software development.

3.4.3.2 Aspect orientation

A program can contain tasks that occur in several separate locations within the code. If activities have to be logged, specific code must be included before and after the activity. If the logging is designed to appear in several places in the program, the developer writes or copies the same code in different places. Other examples include the repetition of database access, transaction management, and authentication. Such multiple occurrences of code are inconsistent with the "don't repeat yourself" (DRY) concept. Aspect orientation enables encapsulation of such tasks so that the task is programmed just once but can be executed in several places.

Aspect orientation implements the principle of separation of concerns for "cross-cutting concerns". Cross-cutting concerns—also referred to as system-level concerns—affect the entire system or technical constraints, and cannot be easily encapsulated. They are not actually necessary to a specific functionality (such as logging).

Examples of cross-cutting concerns are:

- Logging
- Performance profiling
- Validation
- Session
- Synchronization
- Security
- Error handling
- Event-driven programming (for example, PropertyChangeEvents)
- Software tests

Established implementations of aspect-oriented programming are AspectJ, JBoss AOP, and AspectWerkz.

3.4.3.3 Object orientation

In the context of object orientation, procedures are called operations or methods. The idea behind object orientation is the mapping of real-world concepts in objects—for example, a car. This object can also store its data (type, color, and so on) and provides the operations necessary for editing and querying this data.

An important feature of object orientation is classification. Let's stick with the example of the car. A car dealer doesn't just have a single car, but rather many different cars. The class *Car* can thus be regarded as an abstraction. Object-oriented code defines such a class once but allows it to be instanced several times.

If an entire range of objects can be instanced from a class, you need to differentiate between them at runtime. For this reason, each object has its own unique object ID that can be used to call up the object's operations.

Figure 3–6 shows a UML class diagram for the class *Car* and an object diagram with two instanced objects of this class.

To specify possible interactions between objects more precisely, there is a range of relationships available such as association, aggregation, inheritance, interfaces, and abstract classes.

With these additional abstractions, object-oriented architectures provide better modularization support than procedural architectures. Generally, it is easier to implement the principles described above, but that doesn't automatically make an object-oriented architecture a good architecture. Here too, the architect has to develop an appropriate object-oriented model and correctly apply the associated techniques and approaches.

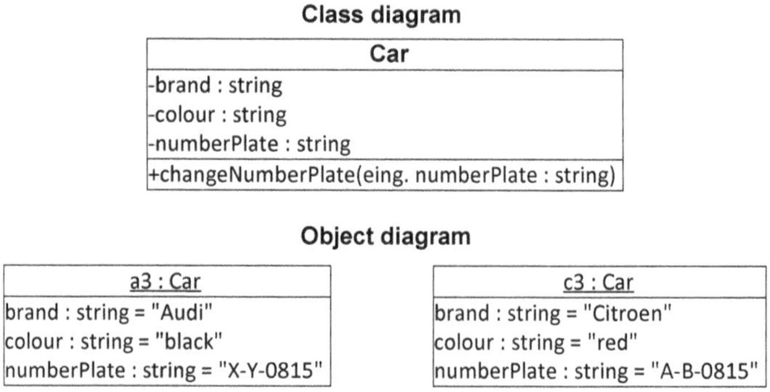

Class diagram

Car
-brand : string
-colour : string
-numberPlate : string
+changeNumberPlate(eing. numberPlate : string)

Object diagram

a3 : Car
brand : string = "Audi"
colour : string = "black"
numberPlate : string = "X-Y-0815"

c3 : Car
brand : string = "Citroen"
colour : string = "red"
numberPlate : string = "A-B-0815"

Figure 3-6   *Example of a class diagram and its associated object diagram*

3.4.3.4 Procedural approaches

A classic (and still popular) approach for the structuring of architectures is the use of procedures. Procedures enable a complex algorithm to be broken down into reusable sub-algorithms that form the basis for implementation of the principle of separation of concerns.

Many programming languages such as *C* or *Cobol* are based on procedures, and object-oriented systems (such as Java static methods) also support procedural abstractions.

3.5   Techniques for a good design

In addition to the architecture principles already presented, there are specific techniques for achieving a good design that a software architect should know. An important challenge in the design of software architectures is effective management of the interdependencies of the individual software building blocks. Sometimes dependencies cannot be avoided, and sometimes they are even advantageous—for example, if a message has to be sent to another class, or a specific method from a different subsystem has to be called.

What's important is that you always discuss designs and keep your alternatives and options open. Models are not reality, and should always be coordinated with the end-user and the client.

3.5.1 Degenerated design

With software that is frequently modified over long periods, the structure of the software can degenerate in the course of time. This is a general problem. In the beginning, architects and designers create a clean, flexible software structure that can still be seen in the first version of the software. However, after the initial implementation, changes in requirements are usually unavoidable. This means that the software has to be modified, extended, and maintained. If the initial design is not taken into account during this process, the original structure can become unrecognizable and can only be understood with difficulty.

There are three basic symptoms that indicate a degenerated design:

Fragility
Changes in one place can result in unforeseen errors in other places.

Rigidity
Even simple modifications are difficult and affect a large number of dependent components.

Low reusability
Components cannot be individually reused due to their many dependencies.

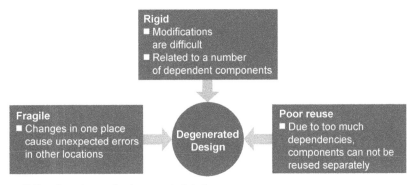

Figure 3-7   *Symptoms of a degenerated design*

3.5.2   Loose coupling

As already explained, the relationships between the building blocks and components enable effective collaboration, and thus form part of the basis of the entire system. Relationships, however, lead to dependencies between components, which in turn can lead to problems. For example, a change to an interface means that all building blocks that use this interface may have to be changed too.

This relationship between building blocks, along with its strength and the resulting dependency, is referred to as coupling.

A simple of measure how strongly a component is coupled to other components is to count the relationships between them. In addition to quantifying it, the nature of a coupling is important too. Some examples of types of coupling are:

Call
A coupling exists when a class directly uses another class by calling a method of that class.

Generation
A different type of coupling exists when a building block generates another building block.

Data
A looser coupling exists when classes communicate via a global data structure or solely via method parameters.

Execution location
A hardware-based coupling exists when building blocks have to run in the same runtime environment or on the same virtual machine.

Time
A temporal coupling exists when the chronological sequence of making calls to building blocks impacts the end result.

Inheritance
In object-oriented code, a subclass is already coupled to its parent class due to the inheritance of attributes. The level of coupling depends on the number of inherited attributes.

The aim of loose coupling is to reduce the complexity of structures. The looser the coupling between multiple building blocks, the easier it is to understand an individual building block without having to inspect a lot of other building blocks. A further aspect is the ease of modification. The looser the coupling, the easier it is to make local changes to individual building blocks without impacting other building blocks.

An example for loose coupling is the observer pattern.

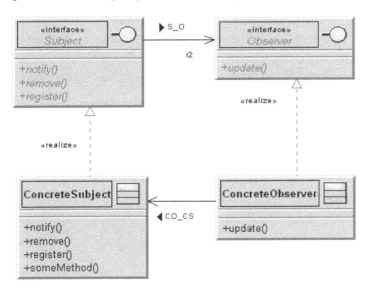

Figure 3-8 *A sample observer pattern*

The only thing that the subject knows about its observers is that they implement the observer interface. There is no fixed link between observers and a subject, and observers can be registered or removed at any time. Changes to the subject or the observer have no effect on the other party, and both can be reused independently of one another.

3.5.3 High cohesion

The term "cohesion" comes from the Latin word cohaerere, which means "to be related".

The principle of loose coupling often leads to the principle of high cohesion, as loose couplings often lead to more cohesively designed building blocks.

A cohesive class solves a single problem and has a specific number of highly cohesive functions. The greater the cohesion, the more cohesive the responsibility of a class in the application.

Here too, it's a matter of how easily system building blocks can be locally modified and understood. If a system building block combines all the properties necessary for understanding and changing it, you can alter it more easily without involving other system building blocks.

You should not group all classes of the same type in packages (such as all filters or all entities), but instead group by systems and subsystems. Cohesive packages accommodate classes of a cohesive functional complex.

3.5.4   The open/closed principle

The open/closed principle was defined in 1988 by Bertrand Meyer and states that software modules should be open for extension but closed for modification.

"Closed" in this context means the module can be used without risk since its interface no longer changes. "Open" means the module can be extended without problems.

In short:

A module should be open for extensions

The original functionality of the module can be adapted by means of extension modules, whereby the extension modules handle only the deviations between the desired and the original functionality.

A module should be closed for modifications

To extend the module, no changes to the original module are necessary. It should therefore provide defined extension points to which extension modules can be connected.

The solution of this apparent contradiction lies in abstraction. With the aid of abstract basic classes, software modules can be created that have a defined, unchangeable implementation, but whose behavior can be freely altered via polymorphism and inheritance.

Here's an example of how **not** to do this:

```
void draw(Form f) {
  if (f.type == circle) drawCircle(f);
  else if (f.type == square) drawSquare(f);
  ...
```

This example is not open for extensions. If you want to draw additional shapes, the source code of drawing method would have to be modified. A better approach would be to move the drawing of the shape into the actual shape class.

3.5.5   Dependency inversion

The principle of dependency inversion states that you should not permit any direct dependencies, but instead only dependencies of abstractions. This ultimately makes it easier to replace building blocks. You should decouple direct dependencies between classes using methods such as the factory method. One of the core reasons (not the only, obviously) for using a dependency inversion is an architectural style with which it makes it very easy to write mocked unit tests, thus making a TDD approach more viable.

Let's look at an example. Assume that you want to develop a Windows application that reads the weather forecast from the Internet and displays its graphically. On the basis of the principles described above, you relocate the functionality that takes care of the handling of the Windows API into a separate library.

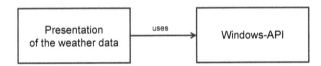

Figure 3-9   *A sample Windows application*

The module for displaying the weather data is now dependent on the Windows API, but the API is not dependent on the display of the weather data. The Windows API can also be used in other applications. However, you can only run your weather display application under Windows. In its current form it won't run on a Mac or in a Linux environment.

This problem can be solved with the aid of an abstract operating system module. This module specifies which functionality the specific implementations have to provide. In this case, the operating system abstraction is not dependent on the specific implementation. You can add a further implementation (for example, for Solaris) without any problems.

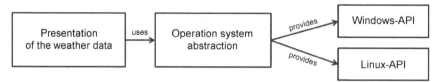

Figure 3-10 *Dependency inversion*

3.5.6   Separation of interfaces

In the case of multiple use of an extensive interface, it can be useful to separate the interface into several more specific interfaces based on:

    Semantic context, or
    The area of responsibility

This type of separation reduces the number of dependent users and thus also the number of possible consequent changes. Furthermore, a number of smaller, more focused interfaces are easier to implement and maintain.

3.5.7   Resolving cyclic dependencies

Cyclic dependencies make it more difficult to maintain and modify systems, and prevent separate reuse.

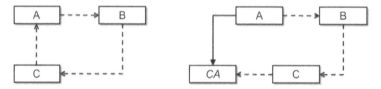

Figure 3-11 *Cyclic dependency*

Unfortunately, cyclic dependencies can't always be avoided. However, in the example shown above, you can do the following:

1. Separate out the parts of A that are used by C in the form of abstraction CA.
2. The cyclic dependency is dissolved by means of an inheritance relationship from A to the abstraction CA.

3.5.8   Liskov's substitution principle

The Liskov substitution principle is named after Barbara Liskov, and was originally defined as follows:

Let q(x) be a provable property of objects x of type T. Then q(y) should be provable for objects y of type S, where S is a subtype of T.

This principle states that a basic class should always be capable of being replaced by its derived classes (subclasses). In such a case the subclass should behave in exactly the same way as its parent class.

If a class does not comply with this principle, it's quite likely that it uses inheritance incorrectly in terms of generalization/specialization.

The capability of many programming languages to overwrite methods can be potentially problematic. If the method's signature is changed—for example, by changing visibility from public to private—or a method suddenly no longer throws exceptions, unwanted behavior can result and the substitution principle is then violated.

An example for violation of this principle, which at first glance is not so obvious, is to model a square as a subclass of rectangle—in other words, the square inherits all the attributes and methods of the rectangle.

Figure 3-12   *A square as a subclass of a rectangle*

First of all we notice that a square only requires a single attribute, namely the length of its sides. A square, however, can also be defined using two side lengths, which then requires you to check that the property of a square (i.e., all sides of equal length) is fulfilled. To do this, the methods setHeight and setWidth have to be modified so that they set the height and width of the square to the same value.

Initially, this doesn't appear to be a problem. A crucial problem first arises in the use of a square in place of a rectangle, since a rectangle cannot always be replaced by a square. For example: A picture is to be given a rectangular frame. The client passes the height and width of the picture, the coordinates of its top left-hand corner, and a square (not a rectangle) to the `drawFrame` method. The `drawFrame` method now calls the `setHeight` and `setWidth` operations of the square, and the result is a square with the side length equal to the width of the picture. This is because the `setWidth` method sets the width and height of the square to the same value.

3.6   Architectural patterns

Patterns are an important instrument in the design and development of software. Patterns exist in many areas of software development—for example, design patterns, architectural patterns, analysis patterns, software organization patterns, and pedagogic patterns.

The classification of architectural patterns takes place in accordance with Frank Buschmann's system of four categories. The underlying concept is to use the problem addressed by the pattern as the basis for the classification.

3.6.1   Adaptable systems

Patterns in this category support the extension of applications and their adaptation to evolving technologies and changing functional requirements.

3.6.1.1 Dependency Injection

In object-oriented design, problems often occur due to the necessity of creating a concrete instance of an abstract interface.

Who manages the lifecycle of the instances used?
Who decides which specific class shall ultimately be instanced at runtime?

This pattern provides an independent building block for this purpose, namely: the assembler.

The assembler determines at runtime how to address the questions listed above. The assembler passes references to specific instances of the dependent objects. It can be regarded as a type of "universal factory".

It first inspects `ServiceUser` for necessary dependencies (Service) and, via meta-information, generates or determines a `ServiceImplementation` that offers the required service. It then "injects" this service implementation into `ServiceUser` and thus decouples the classes from their dependencies.

Established Java implementations for dependency injection are:

JEE 6: Contexts and Dependency Injection (JSR-299)
The Spring Framework

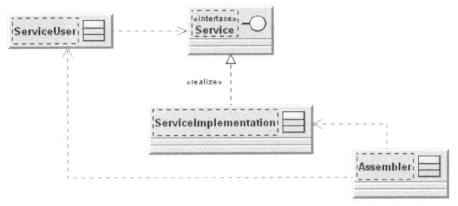

Figure 3-13 *Dependency injection*

3.6.2 Interactive systems

Interactive system patterns support the structuring of interactive software systems.

3.6.2.1 Model-view-controller pattern

Porting of an application to a different platform should not result in restructuring of the entire application. Here, the aim is simple changes or extension and reuse of individual components.

User interfaces change frequently. The same information has to be provided in different ways in different windows, resulting in complexity in the required frameworks. Various groups of users require different layouts or formats. It is difficult to strike a balance between consistent views of a model and performance problems caused by excessive updates.

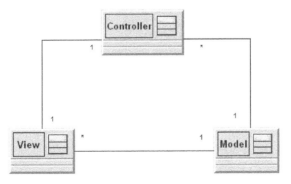

Figure 3-14 *Model-view-controller*

To solve this problem, the user interface is divided into three areas of responsibility. The model encapsulates the normally stable business logic and its data. View components provide views of the model. The controller processes user events, executes the corresponding business logic, and triggers updates of the view components.

A good example of this approach is a spreadsheet program that provides a detailed tabular view and an easily digestible chart view of the same data model.

3.6.2.2 Model-view-presenter pattern

Model-view-presenter (MVP) is an architectural pattern for interactive software systems with user interface-oriented applications. It is based on the model-view-controller pattern and focuses on strict separation of the user interface and business logic (separation of the view and the model). The principle behind this pattern is that applications are broken down into three components:

The model contains the business logic and all of the data required by the view. It is controlled solely by the presenter and knows neither the view nor the presenter.

The view represents the presentation layer and has an extremely simple design. It contains absolutely no control logic, and is solely responsible for the presentation and the receipt of user input.

The presenter links the view to the model and controls the logical flow between the layers. It collects all application use cases, accepts user input from the view, calls methods in the model, and sets the data in the view.

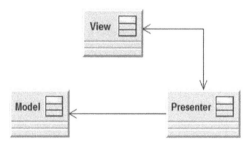

Figure 3-15   *Model-view-presenter*

Due to the simple construction of the presentation layer, views can be replaced by other views. This way, systems can be modified so that they can be used on different platforms and, compared with MVC, are easy to test. Since its definition by Martin Fowler in 2004, MVP has been used for the development of rich clients.

In contrast to MVC, the view in MVP has absolutely no relationships with the model, since the interaction with the model is strictly controlled via the presenter. This results in a slightly different distribution of responsibilities among the three components. In an MVP situation, the model is provided to the presenter via an interface. In contrast, due the absence of an interface, the MVC model is more strongly coupled to the controller. Using the MVC approach, the view knows the model and enables data synchronization. With a passive MVP view, the presenter takes over data binding, and the view does not know the model. In addition, the MVC has no interface and is thus more difficult to replace.

3.6.2.3 Presentation-abstraction-control

Increasing application functionality also increases the complexity of the user interfaces. With complex user interfaces, different areas of functionality can become intermingled, which reduces maintainability. In addition, simple decomposition (as found in the MVC pattern) results, among other things, in unsatisfactory response times when all user events are processed by a single controller.

In this pattern, the structure of the user interface is broken down into hierarchically cooperative "agents". Basic functionality is used by intermediate levels that then provide functionalities for the individual, bottom-level elements of the user interface. Each agent consists of a controller, abstraction, and the view. The controller is the agent's interface to the next higher- and lower-level agents in the hierarchy, and controls its area of responsibility. The abstraction adapts parts of a complete model into a local model that only includes the elements required for the local views. This strictly hierarchical separation enables parallelization of processing operations within the user interface, especially if only parts of the complete model are available.

The Eclipse IDE is a good example: The workbench offers a menu bar, a toolbar, a working area, and a status bar. Perspectives offer these for use as embedded operating elements limited to each perspective's subject area. These include areas for margin views and editor windows, which are then filled by specific content editors and views with menu entries of their own.

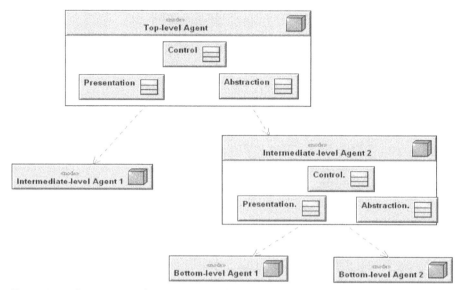

Figure 3-16   *Presentation-abstraction-control*

3.6.3   From chaos to structure

Patterns in this category serve to avoid a mess of components and objects. In particular, they provide support for decomposition of a high-level system task into cooperative subtasks.

3.6.3.1 Layered architecture

This pattern assists in the structuring of large applications. The focus is on the development of a complex system whose dominant characteristic is a mixture of complex services that build on one another.

Dependent high- and low-level operations form functions that access each other, but that can be subdivided into layers with the same level of abstraction. To achieve reusability and/or portability, subdivision takes place into closed layers, so that the effects of subsequent changes only affect that layer.

The solution to the problem lies in stacking the system in horizontal layers that encapsulate operations on the same level of abstraction. The level of abstraction increases with the number of lower layers. Information exchange takes place via interfaces referred to as services. A higher layer uses service provided by the layer below it. Communication across multiple layers is not permitted. This separation results in specialization of the individual layers in specific process aspects such as data storage or user interaction.

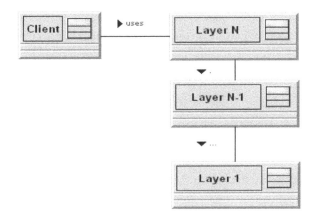

Figure 3-17   *Layered architecture*

This simple concept reduces the number of possible dependencies between components and provides increased reusability. However, it can also result in increased overhead if a layer merely passes requests for provision of specific services to the next layer. Furthermore, changes such as adding a data field have a vertical effect on all layers.

Performance issues can be resolved by skipping over specific layers, although this once again creates additional dependencies.

3.6.3.2 Pipes and filters

The pipes-and-filters architectural pattern is based on a sequence of processing units (filters) that are connected to each other via data channels (pipes). Each filter forwards its results directly to the next filter. The pipes transport the intermediate results from one filter to the next, which involves decoupling of various aspects of the process:

- Chronologically (direct or time-shifted)
- Transport mechanism/format
- Dynamic determination of the next filter:
  parallelism, load sharing, optional filters

Figure 3-18   *Pipes and filters*

The filters are not aware of each other, and can be combined in any sequence via the pipes, thus providing a high level of reusability for the individual pipes and filters. The downside is that that error states that occur during processing are difficult to deal with.

Typical examples of use for this architectural pattern are:

Compilers with stepwise processing and forwarding of the result following each processing step. Typical phases are lexical analysis, parsers, and code generators.

Digital signal processing with the following filters:

Image acquisition, color correction, image effects, and compression, which all forward digital image data to each other.

3.6.3.3 Blackboard

Several specialized subsystems make their knowledge available for creation of a potentially incomplete or approximate solution.

Figure 3–19 shows a UML diagram of the blackboard pattern.

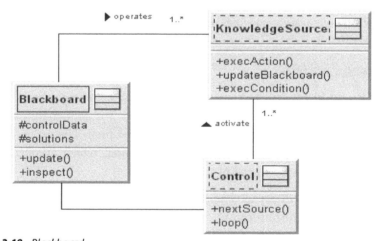

Figure 3-19   *Blackboard*

The elements of a blackboard are:

One or more independent KnowledgeSources that analyze the problem from a particular point of view and send solution proposals to the Blackboard

A central Blackboard that manages the solution approaches or solution elements of the KnowledgeSources

A control component that monitors the `Blackboard` and, where necessary, controls the execution of the `KnowledgeSources`

Examples for the use of the blackboard pattern are software systems for image processing, image recognition, voice recognition, and system monitoring.

3.6.4 Distributed systems

Patterns in this category make statements on proven forms of task distribution and the methods with which subsystems communicate with each other.

3.6.4.1 Broker

Current developments in the software industry have resulted in new application requirements. The software must be capable of running on a distributed system, but must remain unaffected by the continual structural modifications that take place in such systems.

The resources that the applications need to access can be distributed at will, so it has to be possible for the individual software components to access these distributed resources. Transparency is key in such situations. For an individual component, only the availability of a used service is relevant, and it doesn't matter where the service is physically provided within the system. An additional factor is that systems are subject to continuous modification processes. This means that the components involved in a process may well change at runtime.

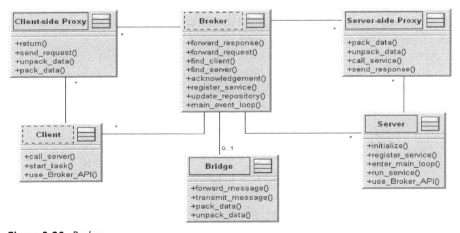

Figure 3-20 Broker

The application must compensate for this with appropriate measures. It is essential to avoid situations in which the application user has to (or can) become involved with the details of the architecture.

In the architecture model of a distributed application, a "broker" component is introduced. This serves as a kind of switching center for communication between servers and clients. The broker component is the central point of communication. Each server independently registers itself with the broker. For each service to be provided by a server, a corresponding service interface is implemented on that server, and these interfaces are communicated to the broker. When clients wish to access a specific service, they send their requests to the broker. The broker then localizes the available server for the respective service and forwards the client's request to it. Following processing of the request, the server then sends the response back to the broker, and the broker forwards the response to the correct client.

3.6.4.2 Service orientation

Service-oriented architectures (SOAs) represent the functional interfaces of software building blocks as distributed, reusable, loosely-coupled services that are accessed via standardized methods.

An SOA defines three roles:

The **service provider** offers services and registers these in the directory service. The **directory service** publishes the services registered by the service providers. The **service consumer** searches for a specific service in the directory and calls it up via a reference provided by the directory service in response to a consumer query. A link is then established to the appropriate service provider and the service can be used.

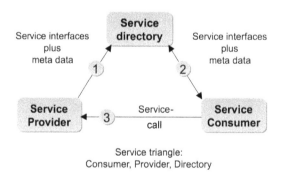

Figure 3-21 SOA

Services in general provide low-granularity interfaces. The term low-granularity is used when a service enables complex functionality with only a few calls.

Ideally, these services are stateless, transactionally self-contained, and idempotent—in other words, no matter how often they are called with the same input data, they always deliver the same result.

Services consist of a contractual service interface (for linking the service consumer to the service provider) and the service implementation. The service implementation does not form part of the contract and is replaceable as long as the interface commitments are complied with.

Services are independent of location, and can be activated at any time and from any location, provided consumers and applications have appropriate access rights ("location transparency").

3.6.4.3 Modularization

Modularization is the term used to describe a reasonable degree of decomposition into and arrangement of a software system into subsystems and components. The core task when modularizing is to subdivide the overall system into components that can then be used to map the logical structure of the application. The aim of modularization is to reduce the complexity of the system via the definition and documentation of clear boundaries.

Combing different tasks within a system increases it susceptibility to errors. Unwanted side effects in areas that are not logically related to the task being performed are difficult to retrace and correct.

Individual modules are created that serve as containers for functionality and areas of responsibility. System coupling takes place via clearly defined interfaces that describe the relationship between the modules. Functional appropriateness, completeness, and simplicity are the partially conflicting goals of module creation.

In contrast to a layered architecture, modularization allows creation of individual vertical systems and separated areas of responsibility.

3.6.4.4 Microservices

Microservices are an important architectural pattern for the creation and integration of distributed systems. This approach involves structuring large systems into small functional units. Each microservice should represent a different functional unit. Microservices are extensively decoupled and run independently. In contrast to self-contained systems that shouldn't talk to each other, microservices can communicate with each other both synchronously and asynchronously. Microservices are developed separately and are put into productive use independently of one another.

3.7   Design patterns

In addition to architectural patterns, design patterns also play an important role in software architecture. Both types of pattern usually present structural and technical solutions.

Whereas architectural patterns typically assist in the decomposition and composition of components, design patterns are more often used to support the implementation of functionality.

However, the boundary between the two categories is blurred.

The best-known design patterns are described by the "Gang of Four" (Gramma, Helm, Johnson, and Vlissides) also known simply as GoF. The *Adapter* is a GoF pattern that assists with translation when two classes cannot communicate with each other due to interface incompatibility.

The *Proxy* is a structural pattern. It controls access to the actual object by providing an identical interface and a reference to the object.

The *Facade* serves as a simplified interface to a subsystem. Subsystems often include many classes and methods that are not used by the outside world that remain hidden. In this case it helps to use a facade.

3.7.1   Adapter

If you wish to use an already existing module whose interface is incompatible with your required interface, the adapter pattern can help.

The adapter is used to adapt the interface.

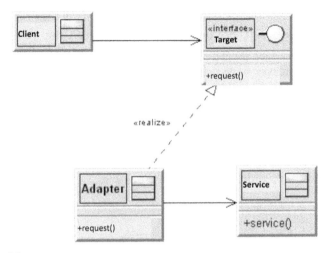

Figure 3-22 *Adapter*

3.7.2 Observer

You should use this pattern if a component should be capable of notifying other components without having to know what the other components are or how many components have to be changed.

An observer should react to a state change in a subject without the subject knowing the observer.

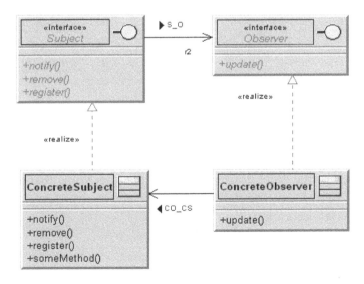

Figure 3-23 *Observer*

The only thing the subject knows about its observers is that they implement the observer interface. There is no fixed link between the observer and the subject. Observers can be registered and removed at any time. Changes to the subject or observer have no effect on each other, and both can be reused independently of one another.

3.7.3   Decorator

A decorator dynamically and transparently adds new functionality to a component, without expanding the component itself.

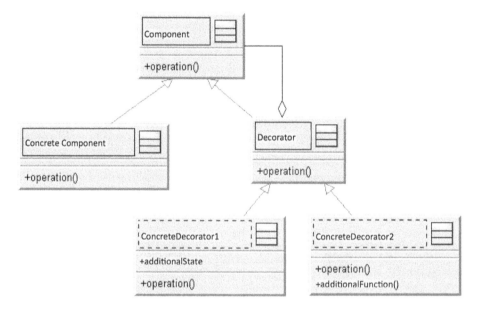

Figure 3-24   *Decorator*

An instance of a decorator is inserted before the class to be decorated, and has the same interface as the class to be decorated. Calls are now forwarded or processed by the decorator, and the caller does not know that a decorator has been inserted. One or more specific decorators define and implement various special decorations.

3.7.4   Proxy

A client has to access the operations of an instance of a particular class. However, it may be that direct access to the operations of the class is impossible, difficult, or inappropriate—for example, if direct access is insecure or inefficient, or if you are working in a distributed environment. In this case, it may not be desirable for the physical network address (for direct access to a distributed object) to be hard-coded in the client. However, without this address direct access via the network is not possible.

In cases like this the proxy pattern can be of assistance. Instead of communicating with the class in question, the client communicates with a proxy. The proxy offers the same interface as the instances of the class to be called, while internally, the proxy forwards the call to an instance of this class.

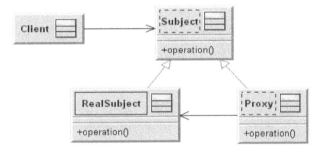

Figure 3-25 *Proxy*

- The **client** is the object that accesses the real subject via the proxy.
- The **proxy** provides the same interface as the real subject to the outside world.
- The **subject** defines the common interface of the proxy and the real subject, and enables the use of proxies instead of real subjects.
- The **real subject** is the object represented by the proxy.

3.7.5 Facade

A facade is another way of reducing dependencies between system components.

With the aid of a facade, the internal components of a subsystem are made invisible to the outside world. It represents a simplified interface to a complex subsystem.

This pattern is useful if, for example, the subsystem contains a large number of technically oriented classes that are rarely or never used by the outside world.

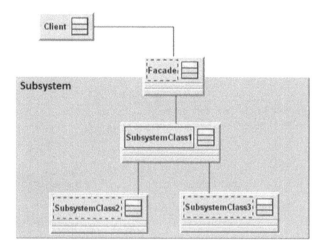

Figure 3-26 *Facade*

3.7.6 Bridge

A bridge in the context of software development is a design pattern and belongs to the structural patterns category.

This pattern serves to separate the implementation from its abstraction (interface), allowing both to be changed independently of each other.

Usually, an implementation is realized via inheritance of the abstraction. This, however, can result in the inheritance hierarchy containing both implementations and other abstract classes. This increases the complexity of the inheritance hierarchy and makes it difficult to maintain.

If the abstract classes and implementations are managed in two different hierarchies, this not only increases clarity but also makes the application independent of the implementation.

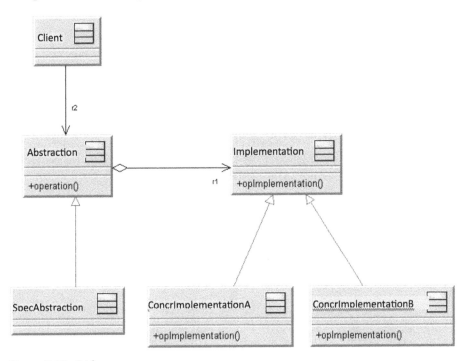

Figure 3-27   Bridge

3.7.7   State

This pattern serves to encapsulate different, state-dependent behaviors of an object. The behavior of an object usually depends on its state. The normal implementation in large switch statements should be avoided by implementing each case of the switch statement in a separate class. This way, the object's state once again becomes an object.

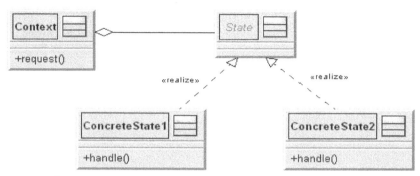

Figure 3-28   *State*

3.7.8   Mediator

The mediator is an arbitrator and controls the cooperative behavior of objects. The objects don't cooperate directly with one another, but instead via the mediator.

The components participating in an interaction are referred to as *colleagues*. They know the mediator with which they are registered as interaction partners.

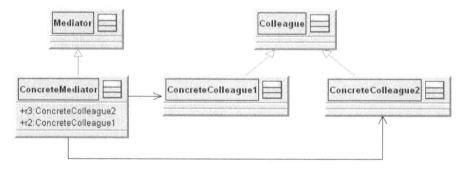

Figure 3-29   *Mediator*

A specific mediator encapsulates complicated interactions between a number of specific components.

Communication control between the components takes place in a single location, which increases comprehensibility and simplifies maintenance.

3.8   Test your knowledge

Here are some detailed excerpts from the *Designing software architectures* section of the iSAQB curriculum [isaqb-curriculum] to help you consolidate what you have learned.

- LG 2-1: Select and adhere to approaches and heuristics for architecture development
    - Fundamental procedures of architecture development
    - Model and view-based architecture development
    - Model-based and domain-driven design
    - Iterative and incremental design
    - Top-down and bottom-up design
    - Influencing factors and constraints as limitations in architecture design (global analysis)
- LG 2-2: Design architectures
    - Designing and appropriately documenting architectures on the basis of known functional and non-functional requirements for software systems that are neither security- nor business-critical
    - Recognizing and justifying mutual dependencies of architecture decisions
    - Making structure decisions in respect of system decomposition and building block structure, and defining dependencies and interfaces between the building blocks
    - Being able to explain the concepts "black box" and "white box" and apply them for specific goals
    - Use of stepwise refinement (hierarchical decomposition) and detailed specification of building blocks
    - Designing individual architecture views—in particular deployment, building block, and runtime views—and their consequences for the associated source code
    - Definition of the mapping of the architecture to the source code, and evaluation of the associated consequences
    - Justification and application of separation of functional and technical elements in architectures
    - Designing and justifying functional structures

Understanding the strong influence of non-functional requirements (ease of modification, robustness, efficiency, and so on),
and taking this into account in architecture and design decisions

LG 2-3: Identify and consider factors influencing software architecture
Determining and taking into account the constraints and influencing factors as limitations on design freedom
Being aware of and taking into account the influence of quality
requirements and technical decisions and concepts on architectures
Being aware of and taking into account the (possible) influence
of organizational structures on building block structures

LG 2-4: Deciding on and designing cross-cutting concepts
Deciding on and, where necessary, implementing cross-disciplinary technical concepts
Identifying and evaluating possible mutual dependencies of
these (technical) decisions

LG 2-5: Describe, explain, and appropriately use important architec-
tural patterns and architectural styles
Data-flow and data-centric architectural styles
Hierarchical architectural styles
Architectural styles for interactive systems
Heterogeneous architectural styles
Architectural styles for asynchronous or distributed systems
Other architectural patterns and styles
Important sources for architectural patterns

LG 2-6: Explain and use design principles
Information hiding
Coupling and cohesion
Separation of concerns
The open/closed principle
Dependency inversion via interfaces
Dependency injection for externalization of dependencies
The relationships between dependencies in the model and in
the source code of programming languages

LG 2-7: Planning dependencies between building blocks

- Understanding dependencies and the coupling between building blocks, and using them for specific goals
- The ability to list the types of coupling (structural, chronological, via data types, via hardware , and so on)
- Recognizing the consequences of coupling.
- Awareness of ways to remove or reduce coupling
- Implementation of relationships in (object-oriented) programming languages

LG 2-8: Designing the building blocks/structural elements of a software architecture

- Knowledge of the desirable properties of building blocks and structural elements (encapsulation, information hiding, limited access)
- Black box and white box building blocks
- Types of building block composition (nesting, use/delegation, inheritance)
- UML notation for different building blocks and their composition
- Packages as a semantically weak form of building block aggregation
- Components with firmly defined interfaces as a more semantically precise form of aggregation

LG 2-9: Design and define interfaces

- Awareness of the importance of interfaces, and the ability to design and define interfaces between architectural building blocks
- Awareness of the desirable properties of interfaces
- Definition of interfaces, in particular external interfaces
- Specification and documentation of interfaces

4 Description and Communication of Software Architectures

Chapter 2 introduced a number of basic software architecture terms as well as the core tasks of a software architect. One of the most important of these tasks is the specification (i.e. documentation) and communication of the software architecture to its stakeholders. Software architects primarily learn via verbal communication what they need to document in writing—in other words, the written description/documentation and verbal communication complement each other.

This chapter provides you with an overview of the tools required for describing/documenting software architectures for their stakeholders in accordance with the iSAQB curriculum.

The following topics are covered in this chapter: Views of software architectures as defined by the iSAQB; template-based, uniformly structured architecture documentation; contents and descriptive elements of the iSAQB views; cross-cutting concerns in software architectures; common document types for describing software architectures; best practices for documentation; and brief overview of selected architecture frameworks.

For the software architectures described in this chapter, we will primarily address the functional (A-architecture) and the technical (T-architecture) levels as defined in Chapter 2. In the following sections, the term "architecture" always refers to software architecture.

More detailed information on these and other topics can, for example, be found in [Clem03], [Sta11], [RH06], and [DE++09].

4.1 Integration with the iSAQB curriculum

An extract from the *Documentation and communication of software architectures* section of the iSAQB curriculum [isaqb-curriculum] is provided below.

4.1.1   Learning goals

LG 3-1:   Explain and consider quality attributes of technical documentation

LG 3-2:   Describe and communicate software architectures

LG 3-3:   Understand how to explain and apply notations/models that describe software architecture

LG 3-4:   Explain and use architectural views

LG 3-5:   Explain and use the system context

LG 3-6:   Document and communicate cross-cutting architectural concepts

LG 3-7:   Describe interfaces

LG 3-8:   Explain and document architectural decisions

LG 3-9:   Understand the use of documentation as written communication

LG 3-10: Know additional resources and documentation tools

4.2   The CoCoME example

This chapter uses the CoCoME application as its main example. CoCoME stands for Common Component Modeling Example (see also [CoCoME], [RR++08]). CoCoME is designed to provide a benchmark for component-based architecture approaches. To this end:

a) A publicly accessible implementation of the application is available. It includes both an information system and an embedded system. The implementation attempts to realize current architecture approaches (such as layered and bus architectures) but nonetheless remains small enough to make it simple to understand.

b) A UML-based description of the CoCoME architecture is also available. The views defined by the authors have also been used for the architecture description.

In [RR++08] more than 15 individual groups describe the application, in each case using their specific architecture approach. This provides an excellent basis for comparing the different architecture approaches.

From our point of view, CoCoME is well-suited for illustrating the concepts and approaches introduced in the following sections. We begin with a short introduction to the application.

4.2.1   Use cases in the CoCoME system

CoCoME is an application system for a supermarket chain. Its first major task is to cover the core functionalities of the supermarket checkouts (see figure 4-1). These are the actual sale at the checkout (with use case UC 1: ProcessSale) and the automated reconfiguration of the checkouts. If in the past 60 minutes more than 50 % of all sales were comprised of less than eight products and the customer paid cash, then the checkout reconfigures itself to become an express checkout (UC 2: ManageExpressCheckout). This means the customer can then only use that checkout with a maximum of eight products and must pay cash.

CoCoME's other major task includes use cases for the management of goods in stock—for example, price management (UC 7: ChangePrice). UC 5: ShowStockReports provides an overview of the goods in stock in the supermarket. UC 3: OrderProducts enables ordering of goods, and UC 4: ReceiveOrderedProducts is used to accept delivered goods into the supermarket's warehouse.

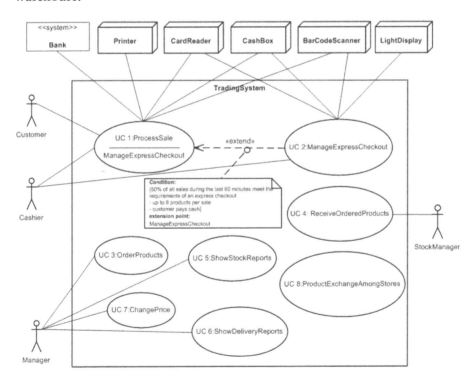

Figure 4-1   *Central use cases in the CoCoME system*

Since a chain of supermarkets is involved, there are also use cases that operate at company level (i.e., beyond the boundaries of the individual supermarket). For example, UC 8: ProductExchangeAmongStores makes suggestions for relocating stocks if specific products start running out in one supermarket, while there are sufficient stocks available in others. UC 6: ShowDeliveryReports provides information on the times required by different suppliers to deliver goods.

4.2.2   Overview of the structure of the CoCoME system

As shown in figure 4-2, the CoCoME system is structured hierarchically on three levels: checkout, supermarket, and supermarket chain. The checkout is connected to a number of external hardware components that it controls (printer, card reader, cash till, barcode reader, express lamp). The checkout also has an interface to banking providers for card payments.

All checkouts are connected to a central server where the supermarket's merchandise management takes place. If, however, the link between checkouts and the supermarket server goes down, the checkout must not stop providing its service. The checkouts are therefore designed so that they can operate autonomously if necessary. This means the checkouts have to manage a local copy of the product and price data. In addition, they also have to temporarily store relevant data on goods sold and synchronize themselves with the server at predefined points in time.

The same naturally also applies to the connection to the chain's central server. This server monitors goods received and sales in the individual stores, controls the logistics at company level, and manages suppliers. If, however, the link to the company server should be temporarily down, the individual stores must be able to act autonomously.

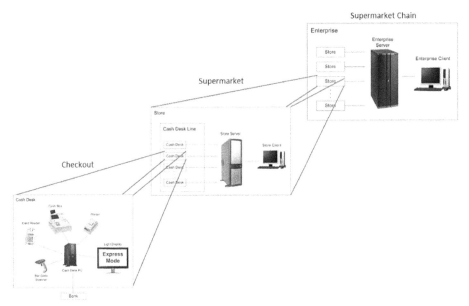

Figure 4-2   *Overview of the structure of the CoCoME system*

4.3   Views and templates

As we have already seen in Chapter 2, the term "architecture view" is frequently used in the context of software architecture descriptions. An architecture view is a representation of the system from a specific viewpoint. It emphasizes important features of the object being viewed, and creates high-level abstractions that obscure the details that are not of significance for this specific point of view. At this stage we want to provide you with an overview and initial guidelines on how to meaningfully describe architecture views.

The views addressed in this chapter (context view, building block view, and so on) have already been covered in Chapter 2. We will often refer to them simply as "views". In addition, we assume that you are already familiar with acronyms such as UML and ER.

4.3.1   Well-established views as defined by the iSAQB

Software architecture literature offers a range of different approaches to describing software architectures, many of which use the concept of views.

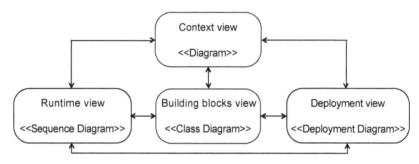

Figure 4-3   *Proven views as defined by the iSAQB*

Within the framework of the iSAQB curriculum, four key views are addressed. These are regarded as proven and have particular practical relevance. They are based on pragmatic software architecture descriptions in line with the template in [ARC42], which in turn is derived from the "4+1" model for software architectures [Kru95]. These four views and the interactions between them are shown in figure 4-3. The views are:

1. **Context view** (or context diagram)
   A diagram with (preferably) UML components, the system under design as a black box, and all external systems and users as actors or UML components. Distribution or deployment context are correspondingly notated using UML node symbols.

2. **Building block view**
   UML component diagrams or top-level class diagrams of the functional and (possibly) technical "software building blocks" of the software system and their relationships to each other

3. **Runtime view**
   Sequence, activity, or similar diagrams for illustration of the main (or key) sequences, in particular those between the building blocks that make up (or lie within) the software systems

4. Deployment view (or infrastructure view)

Deployment of system software artifacts to computer nodes, networks, and so on—in other words, mapping of the software to the physical technical infrastructure

These four views often provide an adequate basis for describing a software architecture. Other specialized views, however, can usefully supplement these—for example, if they enable you to explain things better to your stakeholders. Some examples of specialized views are:

Data view

A detailed description of the database structures of a software system—for example by means of an Entity Relationship (ER) model

"Big Picture"

A view of the high-level system architecture for communication with management (i.e., budget approval)

Mask (or sequence) view

Screen masks, website screen sequence diagrams, and similar

For each additional view, you need to take the effort involved in creation and maintenance into account. The total documentation effort will be correspondingly larger. A detailed explanation of any additional diagram symbols may also be required.

All types of views can exist more than once for elaborating parts or sub-areas of a software system. Their use must be determined based on the stakeholders, the criticality of the system, and the complexity of specific parts of the system.

4.3.2 UML diagrams as a notation tool in view descriptions

The Unified Modeling Language (UML, see [UML-1a], [UML-1b], [UML-1c], [RQ+12], [Oes09]) notation can be used for presenting diagrams within view descriptions. This is useful because—since its standardization by the Object Management Group (OMG) in 1997—UML notation is extensively used in practice. You can thus expect a high level of familiarity with basic UML elements within your target group (you should nonetheless always check this before using UML excessively). As a brief recap, this section covers some of the important UML diagrams for software architectures (which you can skip if you are already familiar with UML).

Diagram types in UML 2

Version 2.3 ([UML-1b], [UML-1c]) was released in 2010 and contains a total of 14 types of diagrams (seven structure diagrams and seven behavior diagrams). These are listed in the table below. UML diagrams that we consider particularly important for view descriptions in software architectures are written in bold type.

UML 2.3 Structure Diagrams	UML 2.3 Behavior Diagrams
UML class diagram	**UML activity diagram**
UML composite structure diagram	UML use case diagram
UML component diagram	UML interaction overview diagram
UML deployment diagram (also: infrastructure diagram)	**UML communication diagram**
UML object diagram	**UML sequence diagram**
UML package diagram	UML timing diagram
UML profile diagram	UML state machine diagram

Table 4-1   *UML 2 diagram types*

The following sections detail two UML structure diagrams and two UML behavior diagrams.

UML class diagram

UML class diagrams show the static structure of classes and relationships between classes. Typical relationships are associations, aggregations, specializations, and generalizations (see figure 4-4). Relationships can have different cardinalities—for example, you will find 1:1, 1:n, and m:n relationships.

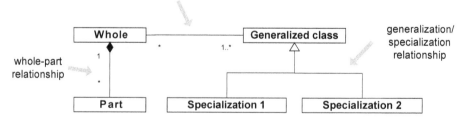

Figure 4-4   *UML class diagram with different types of relationships*

UML component diagram

UML component diagrams provide an overview of the building blocks that make up a software system and describe them using UML components. UML components have well-defined interfaces via which they are connected to other system components. Figure 4-5 shows two UML components that are connected via an input and an output interface.

Figure 4-5   *UML component diagram*

UML activity diagram

UML activity diagrams show possible sequences within elements of the system (for example: classes, components, or use cases). These diagrams can be used to provide detailed descriptions of algorithms, data flows, and control flows. Figure 4-6 shows a sequence with a start point, an end point, substeps, and branching.

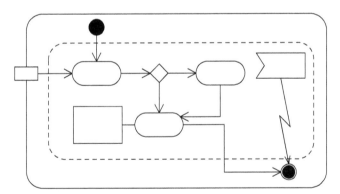

Figure 4-6   *UML activity diagram*

UML sequence diagram

UML sequence diagrams show interactions (message exchange) between instances of building blocks in a software system. To prevent individual sequence diagrams from becoming too large, they can be nested. In figure 4-7, two building block instances exchange messages, and an additional building block instance is addressed via a nested diagram.

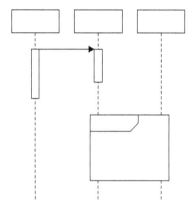

Figure 4-7   *UML sequence diagram*

Conclusion: UML for diagrams in view descriptions

UML is a widely used, extensive tool with many different types of diagrams for describing software systems. You should not, however, regard UML as a universal solution that always works. Don't hesitate to supplement diagrams when it helps your target group to understand things better. Other types of diagrams, such as informal "boxes and arrows", are often used to describe software architectures. It is particularly important to explain the symbols used in such non-standard diagrams.

UML can also be inappropriate for some groups of stakeholders. Other diagrams can, for example, be useful for communicating the architecture at the management level (the "big picture"). PowerPoint slides, for example, can perhaps be combined with Visio diagrams of high-level network symbols and informal "boxes and arrows" diagrams. Event-driven Process Chain (EPC) diagrams for (high-level) process workflows and the like can also be useful at this level.

Correspondingly, entity relationship diagrams are often more suitable for describing databases, while diagrams with network symbols are better when describing administrative and operational aspects.

4.3.3   View description: high-level structure and an example

This section provides a high-level overview of the structure of view descriptions. A template for software architecture descriptions (including view descriptions) is provided in [ARC42]. Such templates can, however, also be found in a range of other approaches—for example, in RM-ODP [RM-ODP]. A brief example is provided in Section 4.3.3.2.

4.3.3.1 High-level structure: template-type view description

When describing software architectures and, in particular, architecture views, it makes sense to use a standard structure or layout. This provides a high recognition value for readers. It's also important to match the description to the respective target group. Ask your stakeholders which aspects need to be described for their own particular tasks.

When describing architecture views, the rule of thumb is to use as little formalism as possible, but as much as necessary. A project shouldn't have to go way off schedule simply because architecture diagrams are only accepted when every little detail has been addressed. As an architect, you should resist the temptation to act dogmatically.

A useful initial framework for the scope of the documentation is the risk level or the complexity of the building blocks to be described. The higher the risks, the more comprehensive the building block documentation will have to be. If the risk levels are manageable, some details can be omitted.

Sample sections for describing architecture views could look as follows:

1. **Brief description**
   The brief description of the view provides a short text-based overview of "what is involved in this specific case".

2. **Diagrams**
   Diagrams provide a graphical representation of the view.

3. **Element catalog**
   - Elements and their properties)
   - Relationships and their properties
   - Interfaces of and between elements
   - Element behavior

   If an element catalog covering all the diagrams is too unwieldy, multiple local element catalogs can be used for the diagrams of a view.

4. **Variability**
   This section uses a text-based description to address the issue of variable elements or relationships within the view. All variabilities in terms of requirements, architecture, design, involved external systems, or infrastructure are included herein.

Depending on the type of view, configuration, installation and operating parameters can also be explained here. A list of all the technological standards to be complied with can also be provided here.

Within the variabilities, it can be useful to differentiate between changeability and flexibility. Changeability addresses foreseeable ability to modify the current system (for example, changing the JDBC database driver), while flexibility addresses the ability to extend the system (for example, by providing extension stages that permit different types of GUI access to the same underlying application).

5. Background information

Text-based background information is important when it comes to understanding the specific structure of a view and can be used to justify specific design decisions. Typical background information includes:

- Justifications for the selected structure or the chosen alternative
- Results of analyses or preliminary assessments of specific content-related system aspects
- Assumptions made in respect of the system, building blocks in use, or the system environment
- References to associated or connected views
- Miscellaneous source information or sample code

4.3.3.2 Example: Excerpt from a view description for a building block view

By way of illustration, an excerpt from the building block view of the CoCoME example is provided below.

Brief description

This section from a building-block view presents an overview of CoCoME for the operation of a supermarket checkout. Figure 4-8 uses a UML composite structure diagram to show the topmost building block level of CoCoME with the software building blocks `Inventory` and `CashDeskLine`, both of which are represented by UML components[1].

---

1 Formally correct UML terminology calls these UML parts, while a UML component is a modular part. To keep things simple we will refer to these as UML components in other diagrams.

Diagram

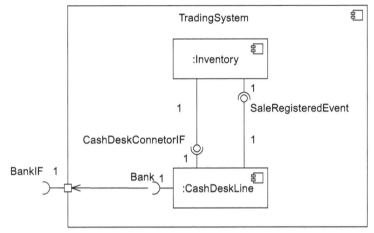

Figure 4-8 *Building block view of CoCoME, topmost level*

Element catalogue of the CoCoME building block view (TradingSystem)

Element	Type	Description
TradingSystem	UML component	The top-level UML component of CoCoME. It contains an information system for warehouse management and an embedded system for the checkout(s).
Inventory	UML part (component)	The component for the information system for warehouse management
CashDeskLine	UML part (component)	. . .
CashDeskConnectorIf	Interface	An interface via which the UML component Inventory communicates with the UML component CashDeskLine. It includes methods for obtaining product information such as description and price. The input is the product barcode.
SaleRegisteredEvent	Interface	. . .

Table 4-2 *Element catalogue of the CoCoME building block view*

Variability

Cash register systems shall be capable of being configured for differing installations. Specific plausibilities will then apply.

Background information

Analyses

Prototypes have shown that the barcode scanner in CoCoME could represent a source of errors. For this reason, appropriate tests are to be carried out during development, and measures are to be implemented in the final system to ensure increased fault tolerance in this area.

Clarification with the responsible stakeholders is still required with regard to whether the CoCoME software should really be configurable down to the local level. Where appropriate, measures for evaluating prototypes are to be implemented by CoCoME test users.

Assumptions

No particular error sources, security risks, or performance bottlenecks can be expected from other CoCoME building blocks.

References to associated views

Refined CoCoME building block view

Runtime views and deployment/infrastructure view

Based on this high-level structure and the sample excerpt of a view description, we will now present the four views listed in Section 4.3.1, starting with the context view.

4.3.4   Context view (or context diagram)

Contents of the context view

The context view (also referred to as the context diagram) is an important link between the text-based/graphical requirements description and the subsequent architecture. It describes the environment of a system and the relationships and connections with this environment, and thus provides all involved parties with an entry point and a map for the system.

In the context view description the emphasis is therefore placed on interfaces to adjacent systems. For a more detailed description of the functional, technical, and organizational aspects of the implementation of these interfaces, reference should be made to the corresponding interface concept.

The following elements are important in the context view:

External actors (adjacent systems and users)

The system to be developed

All interfaces to external actors (all adjacent systems and users) including:

  - The type of interface (for example, online, batch, USB, or file), the data or resources passed via this interface, and any services or functions used
  - Communication protocols used
  - Communication patterns used (for example, synchronous, asynchronous)

On this basis, the context view delimits the scope of the software system in question.

Context view stakeholders

The interfaces to adjacent systems are one of the most critical aspects of a project, so the context view is correspondingly important. Context view stakeholders often include:

  - Project management
  - Requirements analysts (as "input providers")
  - System analysts (as "input providers")
  - Technical or domain experts (as "input providers")
  - Design and development
  - Testers
  - (Perhaps) downstream administration and operations
  - Controlling (assignment of the development costs to cost centers)
  - In the case of "products", perhaps sales and marketing
  - <you-name-it> – (i.e., any others, depending on the organization and the project)

Typical descriptive elements in the context view notation

Descriptions of the context view are primarily made using

  - Context diagrams
  - Lists of adjacent systems with their interfaces

The context view is often both functional and technical. A software system description can thus be functionally delimited from other software systems while being technically integrated into existing or future infrastructures.

The functional element of a context view can be either static or dynamic. The dynamic view tends to be more suitable for test and operations, while the static view is better for architecture, design, and development. In the following sections, we will concentrate on the static view.

It is essential that all relevant aspects of the interfaces be specified in the context view. For example, what is passed through the interface, the format it is passed in, the medium used, and so on—even though several popular diagram types (such as the UML use case diagrams) only illustrate specific aspects of the interface.

Context view diagrams are created using many different notations. If UML diagrams are used, then UML component diagrams and UML composite structure diagrams are particularly useful for functionally-oriented diagrams of this view. In this case, it is appropriate to position the system to be described as the "black box at the center" with well-defined interfaces.

In the case of technically-oriented context views, you can also supplement UML components using UML nodes. UML package symbols are sometimes used for this purpose too. Non-UML network symbols (for example, those used by Visio) are frequently used. Other less formal forms of notation in the PowerPoint "boxes and arrows" style are often used in the context view. The important thing to note is that the representations used are appropriate for communication with your main stakeholders.

The context view provides abstract illustrations of the building block, runtime, and deployment views, so their respective notations and diagrams can also be used to supplement those of the context view itself.

The context view usually contains the following elements:

Type	Description
UML component UML part	As essential top-level elements, UML components and UML parts represent building blocks for which clear (possibly externally visible) interfaces are extremely important. These are the most important symbols in the context view.
UML node	UML node symbols can also be used for (supplementary) illustration of the (technical) deployment or infrastructure context of the software system to be described. For connecting nodes, UML dependency relationships and UML associations can be used.
UML actor	The UML actor type is used to represent the relationship of the described software system to important user roles.
Interfaces to the outside world (dependency relationship)	These interfaces serve to represent the data flow or control flow between external systems and stakeholders. Use UML relationships (dependencies). Where necessary these include information on the interface type, communication protocols, communication patterns, and the passed object type. Each interface should have a meaningful name in the context view.
Legend / Comments	Text-based legends and explanations appear as comments in the diagram.

Table 4-3   *Elements of the context view*

Examples of diagrams from a context view

The following sections show sample context view diagrams from CoCoME, some of which use non-UML description methods.

To begin with, figure 4-9 shows the context of a single cash desk in a simple diagram that consists only of "symbols and lines". The central element here is the `Cash Desk PC`, which represents a connection to a bank and to the various hardware building blocks that form a cash desk. These include a `Bar Code Scanner` for identification of products to be billed, a `Card Reader` for credit/debit cards, the `Cash Box`, a printer, and a monitor. All of these hardware building blocks have interfaces that are addressed by the Cash Desk PC. This PC thus interacts with its surrounding environment via these interfaces.

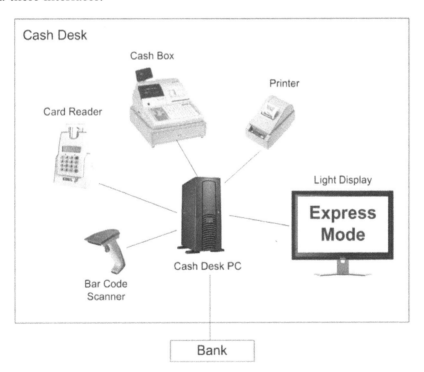

Figure 4-9   *The context of a cash desk*

Figure 4-10 shows the cash desk in the context of a `Store`. At the left of the corresponding UML diagram we see a UML component called `CashDesk-Line`, which contains all the `CashDesks` in the `Store`. These `CashDesks` are connected to a `StoreServer`, which in turn is accessed by a `StoreClient`.

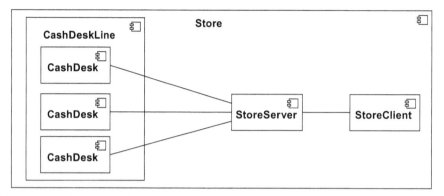

Figure 4-10   *The context of a cash desk in a store*

In figure 4-11, the stores are shown in the context of the company (the `Enterprise`). The corresponding UML diagram shows several `Stores` as UML components connected to the company server (the UML component `EnterpriseServer`), which in turn is accessed by a client (the UML component `EnterpriseClient`).

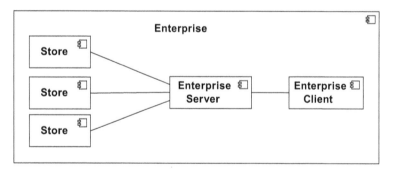

Figure 4-11   *The context of several stores within the enterprise*

4.3.5   Building block view

Contents of the building block view

The building block view shows the static structures of a software system. During development, this view details the desired structure, whereas it has to reflect its real-world structure once the system enters production. The objective of this view is to explicitly show the static structure of the software architecture and the relationships between its building blocks.

As already explained and illustrated in Chapter 2, the term "building block" covers all software and implementation artifacts that ultimately represent abstractions of source code. At the topmost level, these include software subsystems or software packages. It should also be noted that building blocks can themselves consist of other building blocks.

It is helpful if each building block has at least the following attributes:

- Name
- Responsibility or purpose
- Interface
- Reference to its implementation

Other optional attributes can also be added—for example, requirements or open issues.

Building block views can be developed using a top-down approach. In this case, the starting point is a context view. If existing systems have to be integrated, a top-down approach may have to be combined with a bottom-up abstraction of these systems. An example of this is the abstraction of basic services within a service-oriented architecture.

Building block view stakeholders

The building block view primarily addresses the design and implementation of a software system. Its stakeholders are:

- All project staff involved in the architecture, design, development and testing of the software
- Quality assurance (if not already directly assigned to the project)
- The building block view assists project management in the development of work and activity plans.
- Following completion of the software development project, the building block view also enables more efficient maintenance of the resulting software.

Descriptive elements of building block view notation

Typical UML elements in the building block view are component and package symbols.

UML component symbols are the most expedient descriptive elements in the building block view, particularly in the case of systems in which external interfaces play a significant role. Widely used alternatives (or supplements) to

UML components are the classes of the topmost building block level, which are represented by UML class symbols. Classes are used more prevalently during refinement of the building block view (for more on refinements see Section 4.3.9).

Examples of the use of UML components in the building block view are `TradingSystem`, `Inventory`, and `CashDeskLine` (see figure 4-8).

When using different notation types in diagrams, less is often more. Using UML as an example, in many cases the following elements are sufficient to represent an entire software system and its environment:

Type	Description
UML components (with interfaces)	As an essential top-level element, UML components represent building blocks for which clear (possibly externally visible) interfaces are particularly important.
UML packages	UML packages represent a logical encapsulation or abstraction of other elements that will (but do not have to) be specified in more detail at the architecture level. Together with components, they also represent a top-level element of the building block view.
UML classes	UML classes can (but do not have to) be used as building blocks. They are often used for refinement steps.
UML relationships	UML relationships are used between UML components, packages, and classes.
Legend / Comments	Text-based explanations appear as comments in the diagram.

Table 4-4   *Elements required to represent a software system and its environment*

Examples of diagrams from a building block view

As further examples of building block view diagrams, figures 4-12 and 4-13 show refinements of the `Inventory` building block in figure 4-8.

In figure 4-12, the GUI building block `Inventory::GUI` (of `Inventory`) is shown in the form of a UML component. It contains a UML component for `Reporting` via a reporting interface (`ReportingIf`), which generates various reports and statistics. In addition, there is the UML component `Store`, via which a `StoreManager` can be accessed using a `StoreIf` interface (for example, to place product orders).

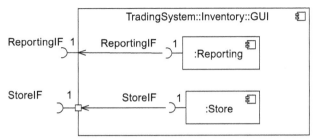

Figure 4-12 *Building block view refinement – GUI for Inventory*

Figure 4-13 shows the internal structure of `Inventory` in refined form. In addition to the GUI building blocks already referred to, it contains the UML components `Application`, `Data`, and `Database`. Various interfaces for UML components (for example, `ReportingIf` and `StoreQueryIf`) are supplemented by important methods such as `OrderEntry` and `ProductOrder`.

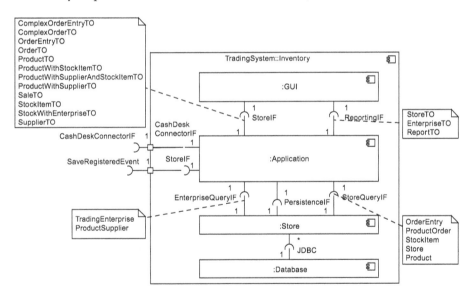

Figure 4-13 *Building block view refinement – Inventory as a white box*

4.3.6   Runtime view

Contents of the runtime view

The runtime view describes the interactions between elements[2] of the software system at runtime. Here, important aspects of system operation come into play that affect system start, runtime configuration, and system administration. The runtime view does not usually describe the entire software system, but instead focuses on important elements of the system and examples that provide an overview.

Note: An exception to this rule is comprehensive use of model-driven software development. If you want to generate code from your UML diagrams that includes dynamic elements from the runtime view, then these diagrams have to describe the architecture of your software system extensively and precisely.

Runtime view stakeholders

The runtime view has various target groups:

   Operators of the software system
   System architects
   All project staff involved in the design, development, and testing of the software

Quality assurance is also a stakeholder in this view (if not already directly assigned to the project).

Typical descriptive elements of the runtime view notation

The runtime view primarily describes the dynamic interaction of building blocks. Various forms of descriptions are used for this, all of which have specific advantages. Some typical examples are:

   UML activity, communication[3] and sequence diagrams
   Traditional flow diagrams can also be a useful notation for the runtime view if they are well understood by your target group.
   In justified cases, small sections of (pseudo)code can be useful.
   Informal verbal sequence descriptions in the form of numbered lists can also be useful. These, however, must be easy to understand and sufficiently short. You also need to make sure that the central semantics of the corre-

---

2   These are in fact *instances* of building blocks.
3   Since the release of UML 2, UML communication diagrams is the name used for the "old" UML collaboration diagrams.

sponding sequence are sufficiently clear, and that the assignment of each activity to the corresponding executing building block is clear.

Business process model and notation (BPMN) is another option for representing business processes in the runtime view.

In some cases, static models are a useful part of the runtime view. For example, if a runtime view of individual instances of objects is to be described, you can use UML object diagrams (or other types) to facilitate this. However, at the architecture level these are not usually necessary, so the focus in the following sections lies solely on elements for dynamic models.

Examples of diagrams from a runtime view

Figures 4-15 and 4-16 show two sample diagrams from the runtime view of CoCoME. The first is a sequence diagram that describes the process of generating a report on current stock levels (Stock Report). For comparison, the second diagram is a communication diagram that describes the same process.

Sequence diagram

Figure 4-14 provides an overview of a number of important elements in a UML sequence diagram.

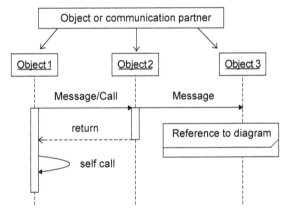

Figure 4-14   *Runtime view: typical elements of sequence diagrams*

Important elements of UML sequence diagrams are listed in tabular form below. Since the release of UML 2, the number of possible elements in these diagrams has increased significantly to include loops, conditions, references to other diagrams, and other elements too. In the interest of simplicity and clarity, the rule of using as few elements as possible applies here too.

Type	Description
Object / communication partner	Horizontal rectangles generally represent objects and communication partners in sequence diagrams. Among other these communication partners can be UML components (for example, from the building block view, or classes).
Vertical broken lines with rectangles	Vertical broken lines with rectangles specify lifelines of objects and communication partners
Arrows	Various call types and messages between communication partners. For example, synchronous and asynchronous method calls are indicated by arrows.
Diagram references	In the case of complex processes, it can be useful to use references to other diagrams.
Loops / Conditions	Loops and conditions are commonly used to control flow structures. They are used mainly for refinement of top-level architectures.
Legend / Comments	Text-based explanations appear as comments in the diagram.

Table 4-5   *Elements of UML sequence diagrams*

Figure 4-15 shows another sequence diagram. It contains typical elements of such diagrams—for example, method calls and a loop.

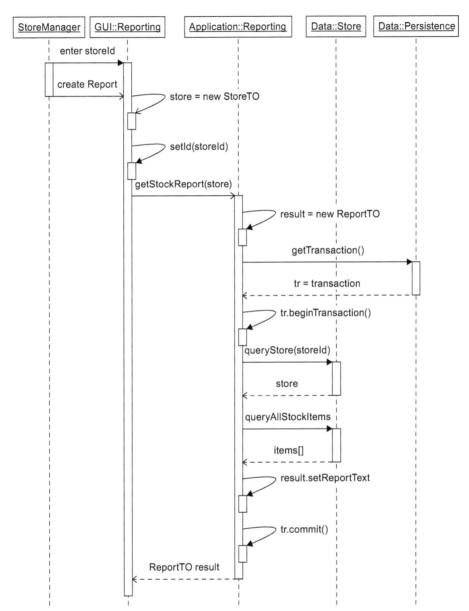

Figure 4-15   *Runtime view: sample sequence diagram "Stock level report"*

The content of this sequence diagram describes the creation of stock level reports. This is a typical CoCoME use case, and describes the following sequence:

A `StoreManager` can use the UML component `GUI::Reporting` to check stock levels. The input is a `storeId`, following which the *Create Report* action must be selected. The reaction is a call to the `getStockReport()` method of the UML component `Application::Reporting`. This in turn accesses the data component `Data::Store` to create an appropriate report in a loop (the loop is enclosed in a transaction `tr.begin ... tr.commit`). As the result, a `ReportTO` object is generated and returned to the UML component `GUI::Reporting`. Finally, the result is displayed as a report in the Store Manager GUI.

Communication diagram

In contrast to the compact, tabular left-to-right layout of UML sequence diagrams, the partners involved in UML communication diagrams can largely be freely arranged. This makes it easier to structure the layout—for example, based on the building blocks from the building block view. However, large diagrams that include many communication relationships can easily become unwieldy and confusing.

Figure 4-16 shows the same sequence as figure 4-15, but this time in the form of a UML communication diagram. The increased freedom available in the arrangement of the diagram's elements is clearly visible.

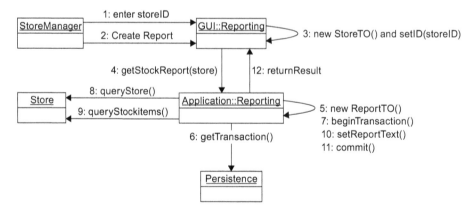

Figure 4-16   *Runtime view: sample communication diagram "Stock level report"*

4.3.7   Deployment/infrastructure view

Contents of the deployment view

Deployment views—also referred to as infrastructure views—describe the (technical) environment in which a software system runs. They assist in the operation and deployment of a software system. In this view, specific UML components from the building block view are placed within nodes in the deployment view. These descriptions therefore contain system software or hardware building blocks such as application servers, database management systems, network connections, servers, and so on.

In this view, artifacts (i.e., work results such as documents, files, software, executables, .war, .ear, script, source, library) are generally assigned to "their" execution nodes (for example, a computer, a server, a device, a database/database system/database management system, an EJB container, a container, an OS, a workflow management system). Assignments of this kind can be made on a 1:1 or an m:n basis—in other words, multiple artifacts can be assigned to more than one node.

An additionally useful feature of the deployment view is the specific mapping of the software system to "reality". For example, this can take place in the form of references to build and deploy scripts (or their descriptions). A separate documentation section may well be appropriate (see also Section 4.5).

Deployment view stakeholders

The deployment view addresses the "real software operating environment". Its main stakeholders are:

- Operators of the software system (a particularly important target group)
- System architects and software architects
- Developers (to ensure that they know the environment and networks in which their software will run and how distributed the software will run)

Typical descriptive elements of the deployment view notation

The central UML entities in this view are UML deployment diagrams, in which nodes can be used to represent any technical elements. Channels (in the form of associations) are used to interconnect nodes. In addition, UML component and package symbols are used for runtime elements (software systems). Here too, less is often more.

In exceptional cases, it can be useful to refine UML deployment diagrams with network symbols (such as those available in Visio) to provide additional information for specific target groups (for example, network administrators). There are also symbols for tape drives, database systems, mainframes, PCs, servers, and so on. These symbols, however, should only be used as supplements to UML diagrams when you are sure your stakeholders will benefit from their use. In a purely UML context, corresponding stereotypes of UML nodes and components can be used instead, assuming that your specific target group is familiar with this form of notation.

The typical symbols in a deployment view are listed in the table below:

Type	Description
UML node	UML nodes are the central element of this view. Other building blocks run on or in them.
Channels / communication paths	Channels and communication paths between nodes are represented as normal UML associations. You can describe the connection in more detail—for example, "1 Gbit/s Ethernet" or "Physical CD".
UML component	UML components are typically placed on nodes—for example, to indicate that they run there on an application server running UNIX.
UML package	UML packages serve to represent groups, sets, or structures of building blocks placed (analog to UML components) on or in nodes. For example, these could be .ear deployables from Java EE.
UML dependency relationship	These serve to represent relationships between UML nodes.
Legend / Comments	Text-based explanations appear as comments in the diagram.

Table 4-6 *Typical symbols in the deployment view*

Examples of diagrams from a deployment/infrastructure view

We will use two sample diagrams to explain the deployment/infrastructure view in more detail.

Figure 4-17 first shows an "enriched", semi-formal UML deployment diagram for a miniature web shop. It consists of two UML nodes that represent a PC that can access the web shop as a client, and the web shop server. The PC is a standard Windows PC with ≥ 3GB RAM. Two Java deployment artifacts, ShopView.jar and ShopAPI.jar, are installed on it. The runtime environment is Java Runtime Environment (JRE) 1.8.x.

The PC accesses the web shop server ShopServer via a TCP/IP link of unspecified bandwidth. The server runs Sun/Oracle Solaris. It has 8GB of RAM and 1TB hard disk capacity. An IBM DB/2 database is used for managing the shop data.

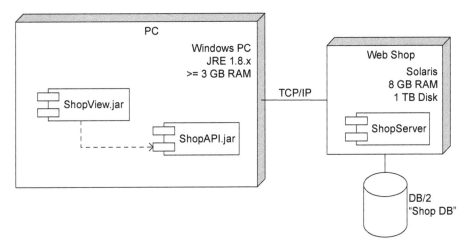

Figure 4-17   *Deployment/infrastructure view – Web shop deployment diagram*

The second diagram (figure 4-18) is a UML deployment diagram that shows an overview of the main physical building blocks in the CoCoME system.

From left to right, we see the UML node `CashDeskPC`. This UML node contains the UML components `CashDesk` (the core cash desk software) and a `CashDeskChannel`. The channel provides communication with the peripheral devices such as `Printer`, `CardReader`, `Bar Code Scanner`, and `Display`. In technical terms, these devices are connected via RS-232 interfaces. The interface/link to the bank is implemented via Java Remote Method Invocation (RMI).

In the center of the diagram we see the `StoreServer` node. It contains the four UML components `Coordinator`, `extCommChannel`, `Application`, and `Data`, along with their UML sub-components. A `StoreServer` node can be connected to any number of cash desk PCs (`CashDeskPC` nodes). Java RMI is the technical basis for these connections too.

A `StoreServer` node can have any number of `StoreClient` nodes. These are also connected using Java RMI. An `Inventory` GUI building block (shown as a UML component) runs on each `StoreClient` node.

At the far right of the diagram we see the company with its `EnterpriseServer` node, to which any number of `StoreServer` nodes can be connected via Java Database Connectivity (JDBC). The `EnterpriseServer` node contains the UML components `Database`, `componentData`, and `componentReporting`. The `EnterpriseServer` node is accessed by any number of `EnterpriseClient` nodes, also via Java RMI. An `EnterpriseClient` node has a GUI UML component for inventory reporting.

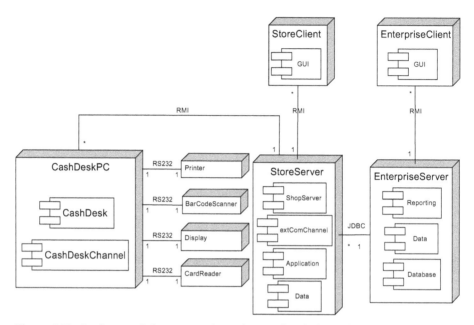

Figure 4-18 *Deployment/infrastructure view – the complete CoCoME deployment diagram*

4.3.8   Interdependencies of architecture views

The design of a specific architecture view often has an impact on other views. Changes to one view necessitate adaptations in other views. It is thus desirable to use an iterative development process in which all dependent views are updated following each change. Special interdependencies should be documented for the following reasons:

- Design decisions become more comprehensible.
- The impact of changes becomes more easily recognizable.
- Dependencies between system components are easier to understand.

The following interdependencies exist between architecture views:

- The context views that let the software system interact as a black box with its neighbors.
- The building block view and the runtime view are derived from the context view, and have relationships with one another (i.e., building blocks interact at runtime).
- The deployment/infrastructure view also exists in a (technical) context. The elements of the building block view are placed within the technical nodes and elements of the deployment/infrastructure view.

4.3.9   Hierarchical refinement of architecture views

Generally speaking, the architecture level represents a "top-level" description of a software system. It primarily serves two purposes: Firstly, such a description should offer an overall impression of the system as a basis for subsequent, more detailed insight and further refinements[4], and secondly, it should provide an abstract (technical) summary of the system that can be used as an entry reference at higher organizational or technical levels.

General explanations of the terms "black box" and "white box" have already been provided in Chapter 2. We will use these terms to explain the hierarchical refinement of architecture views.

The hierarchy fundamentally begins with the context view, which represents the entire system as a *black box* (i.e., the topmost level). As explained in Chapter 2, a black box shows external interfaces and describes functionality using the principle of information hiding. The topmost level of the hierarchy can thus be clearly assigned to the architecture.

The first level of refinement represents the overall system as a *white box*. As explained in Chapter 2, a white box shows the inner structure of a building block, with its dependencies and methods of operation. The internal building blocks are in turn black boxes that are subsequently refined.

At this stage, the transition to software system design begins, and is actually quite fluid. The architecture can (but does not have to) further refine the white box descriptions. You should specify important sub-areas in sufficient detail. Figure 4-19 shows a sample hierarchy of refinements in the building block view. It begins with the context view, which initially refines the building block System into building blocks A and B (for simplicity's sake, the interfaces to AdjacentSystem1 and AdjacentSystem2 have been omitted in the diagram for this first refinement step). Building blocks A and B are then further refined to produce C & D and E & F.

Software system design begins at the latest when a refinement of the modules or components to specific OO classes takes place[5]. When this stage is reached, the architecture and software system design and development must cooperate particularly closely to avoid subsequent "failures".

---

4   The term "refinement" here is used in the context of decomposition or segmentation.
5   Within the context of model-driven development and model-driven architectures, the refinement can (over the course of several steps) even extend to the code level.

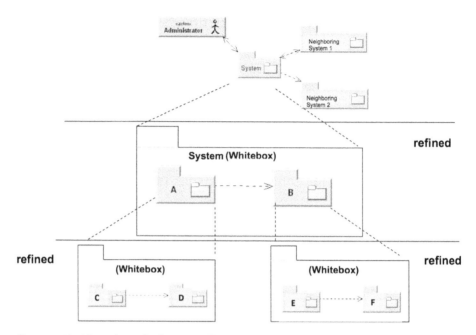

Figure 4-19   *Hierarchy and refinement of building blocks in the building block view*

It should be noted that successive refinement is not restricted to the building block view. The runtime view in particular can be correspondingly refined. In the example shown in figure 4-19, building block A has been refined into building blocks C and D. This could, for example, necessitate a new runtime view diagram that includes communication between the building blocks C and D.

Black box description

For the description of black box building blocks, it makes logical sense to always follow a similar pattern. Typical information used for this purpose is summarized in the table below:

Heading	Content
Purpose / Task	Which (black box) building block is this? What, in a few words, is its task?
Input and output interface(s)	What does the building block provide to others? Which call semantics (call/return, synchronous/ asynchronous, push/pull, events) are supported?
Fulfilled requirements	References to the requirements
Variability	Changes or flexibility that the building block should or can have
Performance characteristics	Quality of Service (QoS)
Storage location / file	Where is the source code for this building block located?
Other administrative information	Author, version, date, change history
Open issues	Issues requiring clarification

Table 4-7   *lack box description data*

A sample excerpt from a black box building block diagram is provided in figure 4-20. This shows a UML component `EmailManagement`, which could, for example, be used as an extension for CoCoME. The diagram shows the UML component and several of its interfaces, such as `Receive email`, `Fetch email`, `Monitor operation`, and `Send email`. How the `EmailManagement` building block is implemented internally is not explicitly shown.

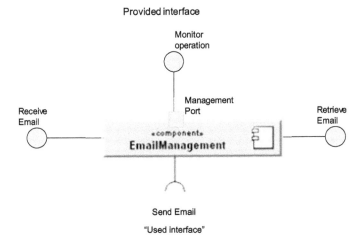

Figure 4-20   *Black box view of the UML component "EmailManagement"*

White box description

When black box building blocks are refined, white box views are created. Use of a defined template is also recommended for white boxes, and the table below details a sample approach:

White box views should be described using a fixed structure:	
Heading	**Content**
Overview diagram	A diagram that shows the internal structure of the white box and a description of the mapping/delegation of the external-to-internal interfaces.
Local building blocks	A table or list of local building blocks. Their internal structure can be described on a further refinement level.
Local relationships	A table or list of the dependencies and relationships between local building blocks
Design decisions	Factors that have led to the creation of this structure or to rejection of alternatives. Impacts of these decisions.

Table 4-8   *White box description data*

For example, a white box refinement of figure 4-20 could break it down into POP3, SMTP, and SNMP building blocks, and possibly into other, self-developing building blocks.

4.4   Technical/cross-cutting concepts in software architectures

The previous section presented views as the central means of describing software architectures and formulated the bases of such descriptions. Additional so-called "technical" or "cross-cutting" concepts will now be introduced in the form of brief concept descriptions (in other words, explicitly not in the form of ready-made solutions). These concepts can be important to certain architecture descriptions, but are not necessarily relevant to a specific architecture. In many cases, pre-existing concepts can be re-used in different systems.

Such technical/cross-cutting concepts cover flow control, error handling, integration, internationalization, persistence, deployment, and so on. We will begin by explaining the theory of such concepts, followed by two brief examples. These descriptions are in no way exhaustive.

4.4.1   Technical/cross-cutting concepts - sample dimensions

As the name suggests, technical or cross-cutting concepts in software architectures often take effect across multiple parts (or even all) of the architecture. At the same time, several of these concepts often have to be addressed orthogonally to each other. Figure 4-21 illustrates this approach by positioning the concepts of error handling, logging, and persistence in different dimensions of a coordinate system. Error handling and logging in particular are often used in most sub-areas of a software system, but are themselves independent from one another (although logging can also be used for error logs within the scope of error handling). Persistence in common multilayer architectures (see [DE++09]) is often encapsulated in only one area, but usually includes error handling and possibly also uses logging.

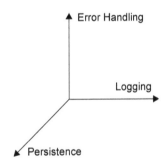

Figure 4-21   *Sample dimensions in a software architecture*

As a further example, in database federation architectures or in heterogeneously distributed information systems (see [CKH05]), the dimensions of autonomy, heterogeneity, and distribution are typical cross-cutting concepts that need to be addressed in the associated software architectures. Similar orthogonal/cross-cutting considerations can in principle be made for all technical or cross-cutting concepts of software architectures.

4.4.2   Error handling

Operational errors, partial outages and similar error cases are normal day-to-day occurrences during the use and execution of software systems. In the context of software architecture, perhaps *the* major task is to consider how foreseeable errors can be handled during the operation of the system. This can, for example, include intercepting formally invalid user inputs, or a "reasonable" reaction of the software to the failure of a connected database system.

Typical error handling tasks that need to be solved by the architecture and development teams include:

Identification of error cases

Definition of appropriate reactions to foreseeable errors, with

Classification into categories and severity levels
Differentiation between functional and technical errors

Minimizing the impact of errors

Making diagnosis of error causes easier—for example, using software system reports:

What went wrong?
Where did it happen?
Why did it go wrong?

Error prevention by the software system, for example:

Early warning of identifiable risks
Permitting processing tolerances

Definition of the technologies for error handling, for example:

C function calls return a status code.
Java exceptions return an error description that includes the above information.

It is (also) your task as a software architect to ensure that end-to-end error handling forms part of the software system, since programs that only work in "good case" scenarios are not suitable for practical use.

4.4.3   Security

Another typical cross-cutting concern in software architectures is security—a topic, where suitable cross-cutting concepts are often addressed far too late in real-life software projects.

Security is a particularly wide-ranging topic, since it more or less affects the entire software application. It begins at the user interface (for example, with the user login and protection against scripting attacks), continues through the entire code (for example, to prevent buffer overflow attacks), and extends as far as the database and its users, who should only be granted specific access rights. These are just some of the many examples that exist.

In addition to the software, organizational measures must also be taken—for example, definition of user groups and roles that have to be coordinated with administration, planning of regular security audits, involvement of employee representatives in the case of sensitive personal data, and so on.

In more general terms, a minimum set of security issues that need to be addressed are:

- Authentication
  - Determination of the sender's identity
- Authorization
  - Granting of user rights based on the user's identity
- Integrity
  - Recognition of manipulation of protected data
- Confidentiality
  - Transferring, transmitting, and storing data so that it can not be accessed by unauthorized parties.
- Non-repudiation
  - Received messages cannot be denied by the sender.
- Availability
  - Measures to counter unforeseen or deliberately caused system malfunctions.

4.5   Architecture and implementation

There comes a time when you have to turn your software architecture into reality—in other words, your architecture descriptions and stepwise refinements are implemented as executable code[6]. Documented specifications and rules on how this mapping should take place are extremely useful. For example, specifications such as "UML component XY shall be implemented as a Java class with the appropriate interfaces", or "We use make with the following makefiles to generate the C executable", or "For our project we use the Java EE code structure specifications and build policies from Sun/Oracle, analogously to Duke's bank example (with a reference)".

---

6   Unless of course you are generating the entire code on a model-driven basis, in which case your rules are contained in your model and in the generator.

Whether these specifications and rules form part of the architecture (your responsibility) or whether you work together with the development team and the rules are created there depends on how the project is organized. Particularly in large projects and organizations they often form part of the design and implementation activities and, in terms of staffing, are located there. In smaller teams this tends to be handled differently. The extent and form of rule formulations varies from project to project, but rules will always help you during the development phase and also during subsequent maintenance of your software.

As a brief example, the following section provides an excerpt from our sample CoCoME system.

4.5.1   Sample implementation

The CoCoME system follows some simple implementation rules:

Design

The CoCoME code follows a specific defined structure, to ensure that the individual software building blocks can be easily located. The CoCoME UML components are each mapped to *Java packages*. The interfaces provided by the components form part of the respective *Java package*. The Java implementation classes of these *interfaces* are, in each case, contained in a *subpackage* that is always called "impl". The CoCoME diagrams can be mapped to this code structure accordingly. A sample of CoCoME code structure is shown in figure 4-22.

Build

CoCoME uses Ant and an Ant build file (build.xml) to construct the entire project. *Ant targets* are available for translation and packaging. The result is a CoCoME.jar file.

Run

The CoCoME.jar file can be started directly via a console using "java …". The Ant build file also includes a prepared Ant target for this purpose. Some basic settings for CoCoME can be configured in the cocome.properties file—for example, the number of clients and stores. Further details on this can be found in the readme.txt file, in the code comments, and in the Javadoc-based CoCoME code documentation.

Figure 4-22   *Sample CoCoME Java files*

4.6   Common document types for software architectures

Normally a series of different documents is used to describe the architecture information covered by the previous sections. This section provides an overview of these documents.

4.6.1   Central architecture description

The central architecture description is the core document for a software architecture. Where possible, it contains all information that is relevance to the architecture, such as:

- The architecture's task, objectives (vision), quality requirements and stakeholders
- Technical and organizational conditions and constraints
- Views, decisions, and patterns used
- Technical concepts
- Quality evaluations
- Identified risks
- And so on …

A template document is a useful tool. For example, the document template in [ARC42] largely follows the contents described in the previous sections of this chapter.

A central architecture description can become quite large, so its description (and maintenance) in a single document may be of limited use. The contents of such a description can be managed using various tools. Some typical options are:

Documents
Documents created using commonly available word processing software are usually easy to use and manage, as long as they don't become too large.

CASE/MDA/UML tools
Modeling tools with powerful report generating functionality can be extremely useful in the creation of documentation (see also Chapter 6). However, you shouldn't underestimate the effort required for the initial project-specific configuration of such tools, particularly for small projects. The major advantage of this approach is the significantly higher level of automation during the maintenance phase (specifically, for repeat generation of architecture documentation), since UML diagrams and sections of code can be incorporated into a new document version without the need for copy and paste.

HTML pages or wikis
"Potentially rather more pragmatic" tools such as wikis may provide a useful compromise between documentation and modeling tools.

Any hybrid forms

A number of additional software tools for the creation of software architectures are discussed in Chapter 6.

4.6.2   Architecture overview

The architecture overview serves as a brief, easy-to-read summary of the central architecture description. If possible, it should be no longer than 30 pages. It addresses similar content, but restricts itself to the essential aspects such as central views, the main quality requirements, and core decisions.

If it is not possible to create a detailed central architecture description—for example, due to the time or effort involved—the architecture overview can serve as a pared-down alternative to a complete description.

4.6.3 Document overview

The document overview is a directory that serves as a per-project or per-application index of all architecture-relevant documents, and that also documents their dependencies. Organizational policies should be defined regarding the structure of this directory and where it can be found. Information should also be included on which documents should be read by whom (i.e., by which role in the project and in what order).

4.6.4 Overview presentation

An overview presentation is a set of slides that presents the architecture (in technical terms) in a maximum of one hour.

A variant suitable for management should summarize the central statements and the business benefit in ten minutes.

4.6.5 Architecture wallpaper

"Architecture wallpaper" is used to present a complete overview of a large number of architecture aspects. In practice, this is usually a collection of poster-sized prints detailing view representations with refinements, quality aspects, and so on. These are hung on a wall or on Metaplan boards, and allow interactive discussion of specific topics—for example, between the architecture and development teams.

Please note: "Architecture wallpaper" is an extremely useful tool for facilitating discussion, but is not the be-all and end-all. Such a large-scale depiction can have a deterrent effect on those whose task it is to implement, test, and operate the software system.

4.6.6 Documentation handbook

The handbook explains the structure and function of the complete project documentation. It is also the right place for explanations of the notations used.

4.6.7 Technical Information

Technical information consists of one or more documents containing important information for project developers and testers. It should be used to store information on development methods and programming guidelines, and on the building, starting, and testing of the system (see also Section 4.5).

4.6.8   Documentation of external interfaces

Special attention should be given to the documentation of externally visible interfaces. These are of central importance to the interaction of the overall system with its context.

Unfortunately, in real-world projects, external interfaces often become time-consuming problem areas. Always give them plenty of attention at an early stage in the project, where you can more easily adjust individual details. It pays to devote more energy to interface documentation at an early stage than to creating really nice diagrams or adding the final grain of syntactical UML refinement in a view description.

4.6.9   Template

With interface descriptions, too, it is useful to follow a consistent pattern. The table below lists a number of typical elements of interface descriptions:

Heading	Content
Identification	The precise name and version of the interface
Resources provided	What resources does this element provide? Syntax of the resource: API, method signatures (e.g., *OMG-IDL, WSDL, OpenAPI/Swagger*) Semantics of the resource: What are the effects of a call of this resource? Initiated events Modified data Changed states Other perceptible side-effects Restrictions on the use of the resource
Error scenarios	Description of the error situation and its associated error handling
Variability and configurability	Can a behavior be changed or configured (for example, via configuration parameters)?
Quality characteristics	What quality characteristics (availability, performance, security, parallelization capability, and so on) apply for this interface?
Design decisions	What reasoning led to the design of this interface? What alternatives exist and why were they rejected?
Notes	Notes or examples of use

Table 4-9   *Typical interface description elements*

4.7   Best-practice rules for documentation

As is also the case with many other procedurally or technically oriented documents, a number of proven rules apply to all types of architecture documentation. These serve primarily to ensure the readability and appropriateness of such documentation.

4.7.1   Rule 1: Write from the readers' perspective

If you don't write your documentation from the readers' perspective, they will feel their needs have not been taken seriously. By their very nature, documents are more often read than written.

Try to avoid excessive use of technical jargon (in practice, this is always a balancing act). Particularly important specialist terminology should be explained separately—for example, in a glossary.

You should pay attention to the structure of documents and bring your thoughts and ideas into a constructive sequence. Once again, we recommend the use of appropriate document templates.

4.7.2   Rule 2: Avoid unnecessary repetition

If repetitions are genuinely necessary, use them sparingly and only if they:

- Simplify the use of the documentation
- Significantly simplify its maintenance and updating

When repetitions with only minor variations occur, ask yourself the following questions:

- Is the variation intentional?
- Should importance be attached to this variation?

Note that documentation from different perspectives should not be regarded as repetition, as it serves to deepen the understanding of whatever is being documented.

4.7.3   Rule 3: Avoid ambiguity

Architecture documentation often leaves future design decisions open (planned freedom of action). However, excessive freedom of interpretation in architecture specifications can easily lead to unforeseen ambiguity.

The use of formal description languages can help to overcome this. These are still (too) rarely used in practice.

If symbolic notations (such as UML) are used, you should explain the meaning of the symbols or include a reference to a separate explanatory source.

4.7.4   Rule 4: Standardized organizational structure or templates

A (standardized) structure is important, particularly when you frequently create architecture documents. It provides recognition value for your readers and simplifies referencing (for example, "See the building block view in the customer management system").

Once the structure has been defined, it should be explained to the user. A predefined structure also assists in maintaining an overview of complete and incomplete elements of the documentation. It also supports documentation quality, since all aspects to be covered by the documents are defined in advance.

4.7.5   Rule 5: Justify important decisions in writing

To support your readers in comprehending your architectures and designs, it is helpful to (briefly) justify important decisions. Justifications can, for example, be provided via references to relevant company policies—for example: "For applications of type X, preference is to be given to the use of .NET or Java EE" or "The customer master data are to be stored exclusively in the central customer database on the mainframe".

Explicitly rejected alternatives can also be of interest, as well as the advantages and disadvantages of a solution. For example, "Use of persistence frameworks developed in-house can result in increased flexibility, but compared with existing frameworks (such as Y) does not justify the associated development and long-term maintenance effort."

Among other things, this can save time in discussions, especially if decisions have to be reconsidered under new circumstances. Justifications help your readers to understand your decisions and why they were made.

4.7.6   Rule 6: Check the documentation's suitability for use

A significant aspect of documentation is its practical, real-world use for your readership. Before you finally release documentation, you should have reviews carried out by suitable representatives of your target group and incorporate the results of these reviews into the documentation. Only the intended group of users can decide whether the right information is provided in the right way.

The review process itself should also be examined. You need to install an improvement process that regularly checks your documentation policies for deficiencies.

4.7.7   Rule 7: Uncluttered diagrams

Another useful rule (for which justifiable deviations can be made) is to avoid excessively large diagrams. According to cognitive science studies, people can usefully handle between five and nine (7 ± 2) elements in diagrams.

Please note: The "architecture wallpaper" approach described in Section 4.6.5 is a clear exception to this rule.

4.7.8   Rule 8: Regular updates

Introduce a process that updates your documentation regularly during development and maintenance work.

Inadequate updating

- Leads to incomplete documentation
- Reduces the benefits and the level of use of the documentation
- Prevents documentation from becoming established as an important source of information, and results in unnecessary enquiries

Unanswered questions demand timely updating. If, however, design decisions change very quickly, you shouldn't update too often; otherwise, you'll soon be doing nothing else. Wait until the dust has settled before you make an update. It is useful to define fixed synchronization deadlines for updates.

4.8   Examples of alternative architecture frameworks

In addition to the comprehensive ISO/IEC/IEEE 42010: 2011 standard referred to in Chapter 2 and the iSAQB approach described in the previous sections, there are many alternative approaches to describing software architectures and architecture frameworks. To help you gain an impression of these (and perhaps spark your interest for further research) this section looks briefly at some examples.

Some broadly used framework approaches for software architecture, or more extensive approaches for enterprise architecture include:

- 4+1 (Kruchten)
- (US) Department of Defense Architectural Framework (DoDAF)
- Model-Driven Architecture from the Object Management Group (OMG-MDA)
- RM-ODP (Reference Model of Open Distributed Processing, ISO/IEC/ITU-T)
- Standards and Architectures for e-Government Applications (SAGA) as a framework for the German Federal Government
- SAP's Enterprise Architecture Framework
- The Open Group Architecture Framework (TOGAF®)
- The Zachman Framework (IBM).

The following sections introduce three of these.

4.8.1   The 4+1 framework

The 4+1 framework from Kruchten [Kru95] is a frequently quoted framework for describing software architectures using views. The iSAQB and arc42 approaches are based on similar concepts.

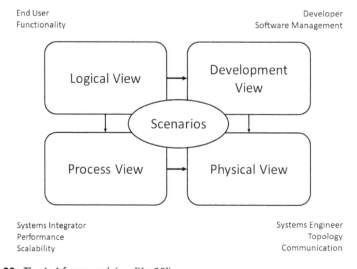

Figure 4-23   *The 4+1 framework (see [Kru95])*

In the 4+1 framework, a differentiation is made between the logical view, the development view, the process view, and the physical view, all of which are positioned around application scenarios (see figure 4-23). The individual views address different stakeholders as follows:

- The logical view considers the software system from a functional perspective—for example, in the form of top-level class diagrams.
- The development view addresses the system from the development perspective—for example, using UML component diagrams.
- The process view is similar to the iSAQB runtime view.
- The physical view addresses mapping of the software system to specific technical systems (as in the deployment or infrastructure view).

4.8.2 RM-ODP

The Reference Model of Open Distributed Processing (RM-ODP, also: ITU-T Rec. X.901-X.904 and ISO/IEC 10746) [RM-ODP] is an established, standardized reference model, used in particular for describing distributed software systems. It uses fundamental concepts developed within the scope of the Advanced Networked Systems Architecture (ANSA) project.

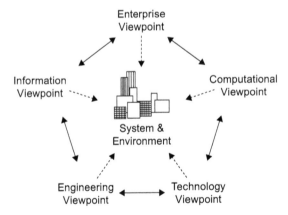

Figure 4-24 *RM-ODP viewpoints (see [RM-ODP])*

Among other things, RM-ODP includes:

- An object modeling approach for the specification of (software) systems
- A view approach
- A definition of infrastructure for distributed software applications

RM-ODP contains the viewpoints illustrated in figure 4-24:

Enterprise viewpoint

This viewpoint shows the operational purpose, scope of use, and rules for a software system.

Information viewpoint

The contents and significance of the data to be processed by the software system are defined here—in other words, the information viewpoint contains a data model.

Computational viewpoint

This viewpoint views the software system in the form of functional elements and their interfaces, broken down into objects.

Engineering viewpoint

The engineering viewpoint addresses mechanisms and functions for distributed interaction of the system's objects.

Technology viewpoint

The mapping, deployment, and interconnection of software system artifacts to and with physical resources are shown here.

4.8.3   SAGA

An example for a governmental approach is SAGA (Standards and Architectures for e-Government Applications) [SAGA08], which was developed under the auspices of the German Federal Ministry of the Interior (BMI). SAGA primarily pursues objectives such as interoperability, reduction of risk costs, openness, scalability, and reuse of applications in an e-government environment. As a German federal government standard, SAGA orientation is a frequent demand in public invitations to tender in Germany.

SAGA includes recommendations for software architectures, and is thus oriented to RM-ODP in this respect. It also includes methods for data and process modeling, and technical requirements (for example, for a secure infrastructure) standards and technologies (for example, for data description such as XML and XSD), middleware technologies (such as Java EE and .NET), and much more besides.

4.9   Test your knowledge

Here are some detailed excerpts from the *Description and communication of software architectures* section of the iSAQB curriculum [isaqb-curriculum] to help you consolidate what you have learned.

LG 3-1: Explain and consider quality attributes of technical documentation.

   Ability to explain the essential fundamentals and quality characteristics of technical documentation

LG 3-2: Describe and communicate software architectures.

   The description of software architectures places special demands due to the different groups of readers (management, developers, QA, and other software architects), and different authors (software architects, developers, and possibly others).

   Awareness of the benefits of template and model-based documentation

LG 3-3: Understand how to explain and apply notations/models to describe software architecture.

   Knowledge of and ability to use selected UML diagrams that are useful for the notation of architecture views

   Knowledge of alternatives to UML diagrams (for example, flow diagrams, numbered lists, BPMN)

LG 3-4: Explain and use architectural views.

   Explain the definition of important architecture views and their importance

   Ability to document different architecture views, such as the building block view, structural view, and so on

LG 3-5: Explain and use the system context.

   Ability to differentiate between the functional and the technical context

LG 3-6: Document and communicate cross-cutting architectural concepts.

   Ability to explain the significance of cross-cutting technical concepts and architectural concepts, and to name some typical concepts

   Knowing that concepts for cross-cutting aspects can be re-used in different systems

LG 3-7: Describe interfaces.

Ability to create interface descriptions and specifications

Ability to differentiate between internal and external interfaces

LG 3-8: Explain and document architectural decisions.

Ability to document and justify the systematic derivation of architecture decisions

LG 3-9: Understand the use of documentation as written communication.

The tools used for the description of software architectures also support their design and development.

The language and means of expression of technical documentation should be aligned to the abilities and objectives of the readers.

LG 3-10: Knowledge of additional resources and tools for documentation.

Awareness of the fundamental features of several published frameworks for the description of software architectures—for example, 4+1, TOGAF®, ISO/IEEE-42010 (formerly 1471), arc42, and so on.

Familiarity with ideas and examples of checklists for software architectures (see also Chapter 5)

Familiarity with tools for the creation and maintenance of architecture documentation (see also Chapter 6)

5 Software Architectures and Quality

Software architecture analysis deals with the analysis of structures and concepts of software systems, in order to evaluate the quality of the software in terms of known requirements. It supports developers, architects, and other involved parties in maintaining and improving quality. Architecture analysis provides an overview of the components in the software system and their dependencies.

As well as architecture analysis, other methods exist for ensuring the quality of the software architecture. These include code and architecture reviews, data and process analyses, and tests (performance tests, load tests, stress tests, and so on). However, we will not be addressing this type of quality assurance here.

Software architecture analysis allows the quality of a software project to be evaluated at any time, revealing risks and enabling quality improvement measures to be derived. Inadequate quality assurance and insufficient checking of the architecture can result in significant risks and losses in the course of software development.

In addition to the evaluation of development structures and concepts, architecture analysis also helps determine the level to which quality requirements are fulfilled.

Architecture analysis and its methods are necessary for continuous quality evaluation of all sizes of architectures. Automated tools can save a lot of time, but are only really suitable for pure code analysis. They should not be regarded as the sole and sufficient solution. Later changes to a bad architecture cost considerable time and money, but architecture analysis can help you address the risks involved in changeability and the fulfillment of quality requirements.

Figure 5–1 shows how architecture analysis is integrated with the architecture business cycle (ABC).

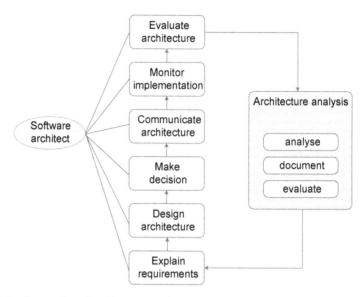

Figure 5-1   *Integration of architecture analysis*

The sub-aspects of architecture analysis can be summarized as a collection of analysis methods, evaluations, and documentations. These are specifically used by the architect to evaluate, document, and communicate the characteristics of the existing architecture.

5.1   Integration with the iSAQB curriculum

An extract from the *Software architectures and quality* section of the iSAQB curriculum [isaqb-curriculum] is provided below.

5.1.1   Learning goals

LG 4-1: Discuss quality models and quality characteristics

LG 4-2: Define quality requirements for software architectures

LG 4-3: Perform qualitative evaluation of software architectures

LG 4-4: Understand the quantitative evaluation of software architectures

LG 4-5: Understand how quality objectives can be achieved

5.2 Evaluating software architectures

A software project involves two types of "things" that can be evaluated:

- Processes—for example, development or operating processes
- Artifacts such as requirements, source code, or other documents

Some of these artifacts (such as the source code) can be evaluated quantitatively (i.e., in numbers), while others that cannot be evaluated numerically are evaluated in terms of their properties or quality.

5.2.1 Qualitative evaluation

Various attributes and models exist for evaluating the quality of software architecture, each focusing on different aspects of the system. These quality models form the basis for evaluations and analyses, since they address the project's quality requirements.

Various sources of information can be of assistance during qualitative evaluation of architectures—for example, requirements, quality trees and scenarios, architecture and design models, source code, and metrics.

5.2.1.1 DIN ISO/IEC 25010

DIN ISO/IEC 9126 [ISO/IEC 9126] defines software quality as the entirety of the features and relevant values of a software product that relate to its suitability to fulfill defined and presupposed requirements.

In 2005, this was replaced by the new DIN ISO/IEC 25010 [ISO/IEC 25010], which is part of the 250xx series of norms. Its official title is *System and software engineering – Systems and software Quality Requirements and Evaluation (SQuaRE) — System and software quality models*.

To ensure success, quality should be continuously assured. For object-oriented software development, this includes reviews, unit and regression tests, and architecture analysis.

Quality models use detail and specifications to make the concept of software quality measurable.

5.2.1.2 Quality characteristics

In the new ISO/IEC 25010 norm, the six main characteristics listed in ISO/IEC 9126 are supplemented by the new characteristics *security* and *compatibility*. Some sub-characteristics were added and other characteristics were renamed:

Functional suitability

Does the software have sufficient functions to fulfill the specified and pre-supposed requirements?

Reliability

Can the software maintain its level of performance under defined conditions for a specific period of time?

Usability

Is the program easy to learn and use? How attractive and user-friendly is the software for the user?

Performance efficiency

How economical is the software for the solution of a specific problem in terms of resources, query and processing response times, and storage space?

Security

How good is data protection? Can unauthorized persons or systems read or modify data? Is access to data allowed for all authorized persons or systems?

Compatibility

Can two or more systems or components exchange information with each other and/or execute their required functions while sharing the same hardware or software environment?

Maintainability

What is the effort involved in error correction, implementation of improvements, or adaptation to changes in the environment? How high is the level of reusability? How stable is the software in terms of changeability without introducing undesired side effects?

Portability

Can the software be used on other (hardware and software) systems?

Each of these main characteristics is refined using sub-characteristics (see Table 5-1).

Functional suitability	Functional completeness Functional correctness Functional appropriateness
Reliability	Maturity Fault tolerance Recoverability Availability
Usability	Appropriateness Recognizability Operability Learnability User interface aesthetics Accessibility User error protection
Performance Efficiency	Time behavior Resource utilization Capacity
Security	Confidentiality Integrity Non-repudiation Accountability Authenticity
Compatibility	Co-existence Interoperability
Maintainability	Modularity Reusability Analyzability Modifiability Testability
Portability	Adaptability Installability Replaceability

Table 5-1   *Quality characteristics in accordance with ISO/IEC 25010 [ISO/IEC 25010]*

5.2.1.3 Additional quality characteristics

One example of a further quality characteristic is scalability, which describes the adaptability of the hardware and software to an increasing volume of requirements. A differentiation is made here between vertical and horizontal scaling. While vertical scaling replaces the system with a more performant solution (for example, by upgrading the server or replacing it with a more powerful model), in the case of horizontal scaling, additional hardware resources (for example, additional servers) are added to the system.

Depending on its purpose, there can be other "characteristics" which are of relevance to the stakeholders as quality characteristics of a software system.

Although they are often regarded as self-evident, relevant quality characteristics should be explicitly documented. Only explicitly documented characteristics can be constructively used to improve quality and ensure transparency. Because he bears the responsibility for the quality of the entire system, it is essential for the software architect to call for explicit and specific quality characteristics or actively rework the existing ones.

5.2.1.4 Effects of specific quality characteristics

The various quality characteristics or attributes of a system can have a wide range of impacts on each other. Some examples are:

- Simplicity increases comprehensibility.
- Security can possibly reduce usability—for example, if specific functions are only available within a specific network.
- Flexibility can possibly reduce testability, since increased flexibility (for example, runtime configurability) can result in a more complex system that requires more testing.
- Adaptability and flexibility in most cases conflict with the requirement for increased performance.
- The requirement for increased performance can in turn hinder timely completion.

For these reasons, you usually need to balance the priorities of the individual quality requirements for each specific piece of software.

5.2.1.5 Tactics and practices for fulfilling quality requirements

So how do we fulfill specific quality characteristics?

There is no universal method for developing solution strategies for specific quality characteristics. As an architect, you have to develop appropriate measures in parallel with the development of views and technical concepts, based on the individual situation and context.

The following sections provide a selection of sample tactics and practices for achieving specific quality characteristics. These tactics often help, but don't work in all cases.

As already explained, individual quality characteristics can mutually impact each other. The desire for increased performance can affect a system's flexibility, storage space requirements, or timely completion. In this case, the following tactics can help:

- Carry out load tests
- Provide additional hardware (for example, more memory)
- Forgo distribution
- Introduce redundancies
- Reduce system component communication
- Reduce system flexibility

This list is, of course, not exhaustive. Situations exist in which performance can be improved via distribution. In another example, increased flexibility can result in a runtime optimizer increasing performance.

As already explained, requirements for increased flexibility and adaptability often conflict with a requirement for increased performance. You therefore need to ask which aspect of the system needs to be more flexible. This could be:

- Functionality
- Data structures or data models
- External software
- Interfaces to other systems
- User interfaces
- The target platform

The answer to this question can help to narrow the scope of the required flexibility. You can then develop various scenarios to check the suitability of alternative architectures.

To improve the flexibility of a system, the following measures can be of assistance:

- Use "information hiding"
    - Hide internal details of a component from others
    - Introduce additional abstraction levels

- Reduce dependencies

- Keep changes as local as possible and limited to a minimum number of building blocks

- Decouple system elements from each other as much as possible
    - Always have building blocks communicate via interfaces
    - Use adapters, facades, or proxies to decouple building blocks

- Increase the understandability of the code

However, all these tactics have their limits and don't work in all cases. They are merely intended to convey the basic idea here of how specific quality characteristics can be achieved.

Another important point that is also worth mentioning is traceability. This is an important characteristic that is indispensable for quality-oriented software development. All system requirements must be traceable in forward and reverse directions—i.e., from their source (via their description, specification and implementation) to their verification.

The following attributes are necessary to achieve traceability:

Unique identification of all requirements

Selection of the nature, timing, responsibility for, and tool support for information collection and management.

5.2.2   Quantitative evaluation

In addition to a qualitative appraisal, quantitative evaluation measures the artifacts of an architecture numerically. If carried out consistently and recorded for extended periods, these measurements can provide good indications of structural changes. They provide no information, however, with respect to the operability or runtime quality of a system. To be comparable, the results of a quantitative evaluation also require a functional and technical context. However, quantitative evaluation of software (and particularly of source code) can help to identify critical elements within systems.

Quantitative methods for quality assurance of architectures include:

Metrics for measurement and evaluation of architectural aspects, such as incoming and outgoing dependencies, or complexity (cyclomatic complexity)

Analysis that focuses on the process (for example, analysis of change frequencies)

Analysis that checks the correct implementation of the architecture (for example, by checking for architectural compliance in the code)

Analysis that addresses the software repository (for example, to detect duplicate code)

5.2.2.1 Checking architecture compliance

Design and implementation are subject to specific limits placed on them by the system's software architecture. For example, the various levels of an architecture restrict the permitted relationships and import capabilities in the source code. It is therefore important that so-called "architecture standards" are also complied with, and that the design and implementation adapt themselves to the architecture. However, checking compliance with architecture standards is not a simple matter. Depending on the nature of the project and the size of the system, there can be a wide range of different architecture standards involved.

The architecture effectively forms the framework (or basic structure) of a software system, and places restrictions on its design and implementation. For example, the logical levels of an architecture restrict the number of possible relationships in the UML design models as well as dependencies between classes in the source code.

There is a range of tools available for checking architecture standards, and evaluating architecture. These tools can be configured to evaluate the compliance of the code based on the predefined architectural standards.

Some static analysis tools are discussed in more detail in Chapter 6.

5.2.2.2 Metrics

A large number of metrics can be determined for a project and its source code. Here are some examples:

■ Requirements
   ■ Number of changed requirements per unit of time

■ Source code
   ■ Degrees of dependency (coupling)
   ■ Number of lines of code
   ■ Number of comments in relation to the number of program lines
   ■ Number of static methods
   ■ Complexity (of the possible execution paths—for cyclomatic complexity, see Section 5.2.2.3)
   ■ Number of methods per class
   ■ Inheritance depth

Software production process

Number of implemented/tested features per unit of time
Number of new lines of codes per unit of time
Time for meetings in relation to the total working time
Relationship of the estimated to the required number of working days
(per artifact)
Ratio of managers to developers to testers

Errors

Average time for correction of an error
Number of errors found per package

Testing

Number of test cases
Number of test cases per class/package
Number of test cases per requirement (test coverage)

Design

Incoming dependencies
Outgoing dependencies
Instability
Abstractness
Distance

System (fully or partially complete)

Performance characteristics such as resource consumption or the time
required for processing specific functions or use cases

5.2.2.3 Cyclomatic complexity

Cyclomatic complexity is also referred to as the McCabe metric (M) and was
introduced in 1976 by Thomas J. McCabe [McC76].

It shows the number of linearly independent paths through a program's
source code and is calculated using the formula:

$$e - n + 2p$$

where e is the number of edges of the graph, n is the number of nodes in the
graph, and p is the number of individual control flow graphs (one graph per
function/procedure).

The McCabe value is a measure of the complexity of a module. It represents a lower limit for the number of possible paths through the module

and an upper limit for the number of test cases needed to cover all edges of the control flow graph.

In general terms, low cyclomatic complexity means that the module is easy to understand, test, and maintain. High cyclomatic complexity means the module is complex and difficult to test. If, however, the complexity can only be reduced with difficulty or the module is easy to understand in spite of a high McCabe value (for example, due to extensive switch statements), an excessively high cyclomatic complexity warning can also be suppressed.

5.3   Prototypes and technical proof of concept

Many different types of problems can arise in the course of a software development project. Either the stakeholders have problems formulating the requirements explicitly (and, above all, completely), or cooperation between system users and developers doesn't function properly. Usually, cooperation ends with the analysis and design phase, since the developers then withdraw and only present the results of their work when the software is complete.

Coordination between teams is very important if they are to learn from one another. Various solutions have to be tested and discussed with the customer, and some requirements cannot be guaranteed based on their theoretical description (for example, real-time requirements). Before the definition phase can be completed, it may therefore be necessary to evaluate individual aspects of the project in a prototype system.

5.3.1   Technical proof of concept

A technical proof of concept is used to implement such a prototype and enables clarification of any technical issues that may arise. It is used to determine whether interaction and cooperation between the technical components functions correctly. Unlike with a prototype, real-world functionality doesn't play a role in the technical proof of concept.

5.3.2   Prototype

A prototype is a simplified experimental model of a planned product or building block. It includes all the functions necessary to fulfill its designed purpose. It may correspond to the planned end product purely in terms of its appearance or in specific technical terms. A prototype often serves as a preliminary step to mass production, but can also be planned as a one-off item whose purpose is solely to demonstrate a specific concept.

5.3.2.1 Benefits and disadvantages of software prototypes

A software prototype shows how the selected functions of the target application will look in practical use. This enables you to better explain and demonstrate the associated requirements and/or development issues. Prototype software enables users to gain important experimental experience, and thus serves as a basis for discussion and further decision-making. This process (known as "prototyping") produces swift results and provides early-stage feedback on the suitability of a solution approach. Early feedback reduces the development risk, and the quality assurance staff can be integrated into the software development process from the very start. With the aid of suitable tools, the prototyping process can be accelerated. The process is then referred to as "rapid prototyping".

As well as the advantages already mentioned prototyping also has some disadvantages. It often increases the development effort (a prototype usually has to be developed in addition to the actual application). There is also the risk of planned "throwaway" prototypes not being junked after all and providing sub-optimal solutions. Prototypes can be regarded as an alternative to high-quality documentation, which is often neglected by the developers.

5.3.2.2 Types of software prototypes

Types of software prototypes include:

A **demonstration prototype** serves for order acquisition and provides the involved parties with an idea of how the final product could look. It is essential that this type of prototype is subsequently junked.

A "real" **prototype** is developed in parallel with its corresponding area of application modeling, and demonstrates various aspects of the user interface or functional elements. This type of prototype is used for analysis purposes.

A **laboratory sample** is an experimental prototype and serves to answer design-related questions and alternatives.

A **pilot system** developed during evolutionary prototyping is already a core prototype of the product. Further development from the prototype to the product takes place stepwise in cycles with involvement of the product's users. Differentiation between the prototype and the product disappears during the course of the development. Because it will probably end up being used in the final product, a pilot system demands extremely thorough design.

5.4 Architecture analysis

In addition to reviews, unit tests, acceptance, and regression tests, architecture analysis is an important technique that supports the software architect in his day-to-day work. It enables evaluation of the quality of a software architecture. In addition to the use of a suitable quality model and definition of functional processes, one of the most important prerequisites for architecture analysis is requirements analysis and analysis of the architecture's objectives.

The results of architecture analysis can be evaluated based on specific quality criteria such as robustness, availability, or security. These criteria must be defined and prioritized at an early stage of requirements specification.

5.4.1 The ATAM method

ATAM stands for *Architecture Tradeoff Analysis Method*. It is a methodical approach to qualitative architecture evaluation and aids selection of an appropriate architecture for a planned system. ATAM was developed at the Software Engineering Institute (SEI) at Carnegie Mellon University.

ATAM is a leading method in the field of architecture evaluation.

Advantages of ATAM

- Explicit quality requirements
- Improved architecture documentation
- A documented basis for architectural decisions
- Early identification of risks
- Improved communication between the involved parties

Prerequisites for ATAM

- The system architect (or a technical point of contact)
- Architecture documentation
- A responsible functional point of contact for the customer

The evaluation procedure

ATAM breaks down the evaluation of a software architecture into four phases (see figure 5–2).

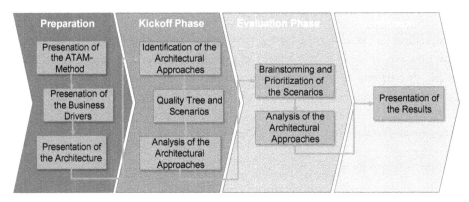

Figure 5-2   *The evaluation procedure*

The first step of an architecture evaluation involves the customer or client identifying the relevant stakeholders for the procedure. This will usually be a small team that includes at least (client) management and project management.

Prior to definition of the evaluation objectives, the kick-off phase involves a brief presentation of the evaluation method to the stakeholders. It should be clear to all participants that the purpose is to determine risks (and non-risks) and to outline appropriate measures. The client presents the business objectives of the system for evaluation.

The responsible architect should then briefly present the architecture of the system. This presentation includes the complete context of the system (including all adjacent systems), top-level building blocks, and runtime views of the most important use cases or change scenarios.

The stakeholders should then compile all significant quality requirements and organize them hierarchically in a quality tree. To enable the evaluation team to begin work, they also need to describe scenarios for the most important quality objectives.

Following analysis of these scenarios, decisions should be classified into four aspects (see figure 5–3):

Risks

Risks are elements of the architecture that, depending on how things develop, can endanger the fulfillment of business objectives and cause other issues too.

Sensitivity points

At "sensitivity points" in an architecture, even minor changes can have wide-ranging consequences. These are the critical components in an architecture for fulfillment of a quality criterion.

Compromises

Trade-offs specify whether (or how) a design decision could mutually affect multiple quality characteristics.

Non-risks

Which scenarios are fulfilled in all cases (i.e., risk-free)?

Risks are classified into themes that indicate how they may endanger the business objectives.

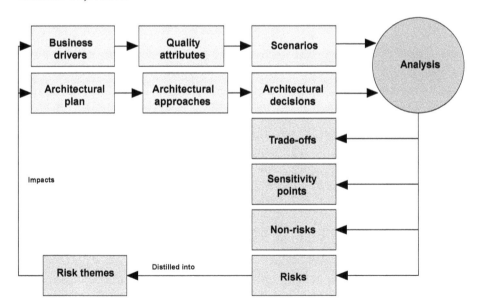

Figure 5-3   *ATAM (Source: Software Engineering Institute)*

Creating a quality tree

A quality tree hierarchically refines the system-specific or product-specific quality requirements (see figure 5–4). Major criteria are located at the top of the tree, while more specific requirements are found at the bottom. The "leaves" of the quality tree are scenarios (see the *Scenarios* section below) that describe individual characteristics in as specific and detailed a way as possible.

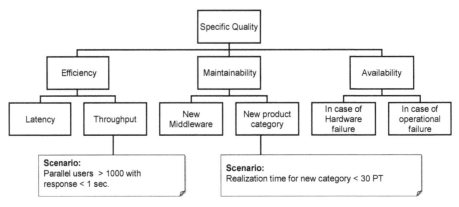

Figure 5-4   *The hierarchical form of a quality tree*

The characteristics and their scenarios are prioritized by the leading stake-holders according to their respective business benefit (see figure 5–5), and also by the architects according their technical complexity. This provides the architects with prioritized scenarios during the actual evaluation.

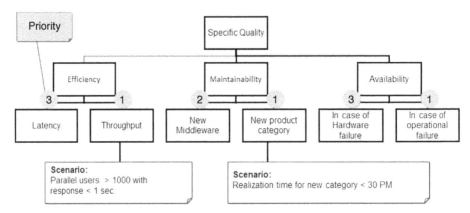

Figure 5-5   *Prioritization within the quality tree*

The evaluation of the quality characteristics[1] usually takes place in a small group together with the architect, and in the order determined by the priorities.

The process involves answering a range of different questions:

- What architecture decisions were made to achieve a scenario?
- Which architecture approach supports achievement of the scenario?
- What compromises were agreed?
- Were other quality characteristics or architecture objectives affected?
- What risks exist?
- What analyses, prototypes, or appraisals support this decision?

On completion of the evaluation you should have a good overview of:

- The quality of the architecture with regard to defined scenarios and specific architecture objectives
- Risks associated with the implementation of the most important scenarios
- Potential measures to eliminate risks
- Scenarios that can be achieved without risk

Scenarios

In an ATAM context, quality characteristics are described by means of scenarios (scenario-based architecture evaluation). These scenarios describe how a system reacts in specific situations, they characterize the interaction of stakeholders with the system, and they enable assessment of the risks involved in achieving these quality characteristics. They are used to specify precisely what the parties involved in the project understand by specific quality characteristics—for example, what "reliability" actually means to all those involved.

Types of scenarios

Types of scenarios include:

- **Application scenarios.** These describe how the system reacts to specific stimuli at runtime. They include scenarios for describing efficiency and/or performance.
- **Change scenarios** describe what happens in the case of a change to the system or its immediate surroundings—for example, if an additional function is implemented.
- **Stress** or **limit** scenarios describe how the system reacts to extreme situations—for example, a power failure.

---

1   Strictly speaking, the risks associated with fulfilment of the each scenario are evaluated.

Elements of scenarios

Scenarios normally consist of the following main elements (quoted from [HS11]. The original list comes from [BCK03]):

- A **trigger** is a specific event that occurs as a result of a specific interaction between the triggering stakeholder and the system—for example, when a user calls a function or a system component fails.
- The **source** describes where a trigger comes from.
- The **environment** describes the status of the system at the time the trigger occurs.
- There is also a **system artifact** that is affected by the trigger.
- A **response** is provided by the system as a reaction to the trigger.
- A **response measure** is an evaluation model for measurement/evaluation of the quality of the system's response.

Figure 5–6 provides an overview of the component elements of a scenario.

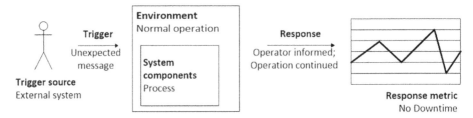

Figure 5-6   *Elements of a scenario*

Sample scenarios

Here are some examples of the use of scenarios for detailed specification of quality requirements.

Application scenarios

During normal system operation, the response to a price enquiry must be displayed to the end users in less than 5 seconds. If the system is operating under heavy load (for example, year-end business), a response may take up to 15 seconds, but in this case a corresponding message is to be displayed to the user beforehand.

When using the system for the first time, a user without prior knowledge should be able to locate and use the desired functionality within 15 minutes.

Should invalid or incorrect data be entered in the input fields, the system must output corresponding message texts and continue working normally.

Change scenarios

The development of new functionalities must be fulfillable in less than 30 man-days.

It must be possible to program and test support for a new browser version in less than 30 man-days.

Stress or limit scenarios

In the case of CPU outage during normal operation, the standby system must be available within 15 minutes.

On failure of a database system, the system shall continue to operate with the specified performance and capacity.

Table 5-2 lists some sample elements of performance scenarios.

Source of the trigger	Internal or external
Trigger	Any event: periodic, sporadic, random, specific
Environment	Normal operation, high load, overload
System artifact	Entire system
Response	Effects on execution behavior (Can the system be used in full or only partially following the trigger? Are functions and data fully or only partially usable?)
	Effects on runtime behavior of the system (How does the trigger affect response times and the use of resources?)
Response measure	Latency, reaction time, throughput
	Error rate, extent of lost data or non-availability of functions, fluctuations in system accessibility

Table 5-2   *Sample elements of performance scenarios*

Table 5-3 lists some sample elements of reliability scenarios.

Source of the trigger	Internal or external
Trigger	Fault, outage, or loss of a system component, correct or incorrect use of a system service
Environment	Normal operation or special (impaired) operating conditions
System artifact	Entire system or any component elements
Response	The system detects and corrects the fault, notifies the responsible person, and switches off or replaces faulty components. As a result of the trigger, the system (or a component element) enters an error state or deactivates the function.
Response measure	Times during which the system must be available or restored The time between detection of an error/abnormal behavior and its correction The period of time in which the system may remain in a state of impaired operation or an error state

Table 5-3   *Sample elements of reliability scenarios*

5.5   Test your knowledge

Here are some detailed excerpts from the *Software architectures and quality* section of the iSAQB curriculum [isaqb-curriculum] to help you consolidate what you have learned.

LG 4-1: Discuss quality models and quality characteristics.
Ability to explain the terms "quality" (as used in [ISO/IEC 25010]) and "quality characteristics"
Ability to explain quality models (e.g., [ISO/IEC 25010])
Ability to explain the interrelationships and interdependencies of quality characteristics

LG 4-2: Define quality requirements for software architectures.
Ability to formulate quality requirements for software and software architectures
Ability to explain and carry out the creation of scenarios and quality trees
Ability to formulate sample software quality requirements

LG 4-3: Perform qualitative evaluation of software architectures.

- Familiarity with and ability to use methodical approaches for the analysis and evaluation of software architectures
- Familiarity with the ATAM method for qualitative evaluation of software architectures

LG 4-4: Understanding the quantitative evaluation of software architectures.

- Familiarity with metrics (such as lines of code or cyclomatic complexity) and other measurement instruments for the evaluation of architectures

LG 4-5: Understanding how quality objectives can be achieved.

- Ability to explain and use tactics, practices, and technical methods to achieve important quality objectives in software systems:

  Efficiency/performance

  Maintainability, changeability, extendibility, flexibility

  Identification of corresponding risks

6   Tools for Software Architects

Various categories of tools are available that support software architects' tasks. This section introduces these categories and provides decision criteria for the selection of specific and/or typical tools.

6.1   Integration with the iSAQB curriculum

An extract from the *Tools for software architects* section of the iSAQB curriculum [isaqb curriculum] is provided below.

6.1.1   Learning goals

LG 5-1: Name and explain important tool categories

LG 5-2: Select tools according to requirements

6.2   General information

You don't need to know specific examples of typical tools or products to take the CPSA-F examination. The examination deals primarily with tool categories and decision criteria (in real life, software architects naturally have to learn to use such tools appropriately, but that is not what this book is about). The examples of tools, mentioned in this book, were considered to be up-to-date and correct at the time of preparation of the book.

As a software architect you will often be confronted with typical "across-the-board" requirements with regard to your choice of tool types. Of course, such tools should perform their tasks comprehensively and reliably, but with minimal impacts on other areas.

In our opinion, there are two other general aspects of tool choices that deserve particular attention. These are:

6.2.1   Costs

Commercial tools are available at a wide range of prices and with varying costs structures. Payment models include one-time purchase for a flat-rate price, prices that depend on the system size or the operating and/or development environment, License price plus regular maintenance charges, leasing, and so on. Selecting an appropriate licensing model is part of the tool selection process.

In addition to the cost of the software itself, you also have to consider administration and operating costs, as well as the cost of learning and training. Training costs alone can far exceed the purchase price of many software licenses.

6.2.2   Licenses and licensing conditions

As a software architect, you need to be aware of the prevailing license conditions, particularly for the use of free ware and open source tools.

Without going into detail on licensing law, the following sections list some of the available options:

Some software licenses permit unrestricted, free-of-charge use of the tool in question, independent of the nature or target market of the system created with it.

Other licensing models permit free use for non-commercial purposes only. Use of the licensed tools is restricted the moment you demand money or an alternative form of payment for use of a system created using such a tool.

Yet other licensing models require the system created with their tools to be distributed under the same license as the tool itself. This can result in you not being able to sell your software, and instead having to distribute it (and its source code) free of charge.

The range of legal options is extensive, and is not always easy to understand or those without appropriate specialist knowledge. If you are in any doubt, always seek legal advice prior to using a tool, a framework, or a library. Most large software organizations have their own license management departments to deal with these kinds of issues.

Warning: In the case of license violations, you can be sued (or warned) by malevolent users of your system, competitors, rivals, or others. This usually results in significant costs and a lot of effort. Always take this risk seriously and clarify the licensing conditions before using external tools, libraries, and frameworks. Open-source tools especially have highly restrictive usage clauses when it comes to commercial use of products created with them.

6.3 Requirements management tools

Requirements management is performed throughout the system development lifecycle, both for new developments and changes to existing systems.

In addition to the collection of requirements, the process also includes measures for their management. The aim of requirements management is to achieve a common understanding of the system under development for the contractor and the customer. The resulting documentation often serves as a contractual basis for the subsequent implementation, and therefore needs to have a predefined structure.

6.3.1 Requirements and decision criteria

- Support requirements documentation and analysis
- Text-based and graphical presentation of requirements
- Requirements management
- Reduction of redundancies
- Support of retraceability between requirements and architecture
- Team capability
- Version and configuration management

6.3.2 Challenges faced by requirements management tools

- Many current graphical representation tools (such as UML models, mind maps, or free-form diagrams) cannot be edited simultaneously by multiple users. This makes merging diagrams extremely time-consuming and prone to error.
- Version and configuration management support

6.3.3 Examples

- CaliberRM (Micro Focus)
- Cameo Requirements (No Magic Inc.)
- CARE (SOPHIST GmbH)

Enterprise Architect (SparxSystems Ltd.)
in-Step (microTOOL GmbH)
Polarion® REQUIREMENTS™ (Siemens)
Rational DOORS (IBM)
Rational RequisitePro (IBM)

6.4   Modeling tools

Modeling tools can depict functional and/or technical models of software and requirements, and problem domains. They assist in creating and maintaining (mainly) graphical abstractions of reality.

Such tools can, for example, provide support starting with (abstract) business processes via stepwise refinement of more and more detailed representations of the respective circumstances.

6.4.1   Requirements and decision criteria

- Support for standardized modeling methods—for example, UML, SysML, entity-relationship models, BPMN, state charts, Petri nets, and others
- Support for informal models
- Support for different views/model types (diagram types)
- Support for static and dynamic modeling
- Model checking (validation, plausibility checking)
- Separation of diagrams and the objects contained in them, particularly with a view to reusing objects in other diagrams
- Linking or concatenation of models and diagrams. Automatic forwarding to the relevant (refining) model elements or diagrams when selected (i.e., clicked).
- Support for explicit meta-models
- Capabilities for manual or program-controlled modification of the meta-models
- Ability tor define your own modeling languages (domain-specific languages, including graphical languages)
- Integration with version management systems (such as Subversion, Git, Mercurial)
- Multi-user capability and rights concept
- Document generation (in various formats) from models. Document layout and structure should be configurable and/or programmable.
- Reverse engineering of source code

6.4.2   Challenges faced by modeling tools

Many current graphical representation tools (such as UML models, Mind Maps, or free-form diagrams) cannot be edited simultaneously by multiple users. This makes merging of diagrams extremely time-consuming and prone to error.

Notations often unsuitable for non-technical stakeholders

Often poor or non-existent integration into software development environments, resulting in a lack of acceptance by the developers

6.4.3   Examples

ArgoUML (open source)

ARIS (IDS Scheer)

Enterprise Architect (SparxSystems Ltd.)

Innovator (MID GmbH)

MagicDraw (No Magic)

PowerDesigner (SAP SE)

Rational Software Architect (IBM Rational)

StarUML (open source)

Visual Paradigm (Visual Paradigm International)

6.5   Generation tools

Generation tools can generate any artifacts on the basis of abstract descriptions. For example:

Class and method bodies in different programming languages based on UML class models

SQL or DDL statements for specific database systems, and test data or data access modules based on data models

Lexers and parsers based on formal grammars

Classes or functions for programming languages that are able to read or write XML Schema based on XML Schema Definitions (XSDs)

Documentation from source code

JPG, PNG or vector graphic images from text-based descriptions

6.5.1   Requirements and decision criteria

Independence from the target platform and the format of the generated
artifacts
Independence from the meta-models of the input data/artifacts
Flexibility of the transformation process
Certification for security-critical applications.

6.5.2   Challenges faced by code generators

Freely definable meta-models and generation rules offer increased flexibility,
but at the expense of simplicity.

6.5.3   Examples

ANTLR (open source parser generator)
AndroMDA (open source)
openArchitectureWare (open source)
Many modeling tools can generate artifacts from models or diagrams.
Examples here are database structures such as tables and views.
Implementation-level convention-over-configuration frameworks such as
Ruby on Rails, Grails, and Spring Roo also belong in this category, as they
generate (code) artifacts on the basis of abstract description.

6.6   Static code analysis tools

When analyzed statically, the source text is subjected to a range of formal
checks that scan the application for irregularities and errors. This can take
place manually or with tool support.

Tools can help with the evaluation of various quality characteristics
(such as complexity) in existing software systems. By identifying dependencies, static code analysis tools can also be used to optimize runtime efficiency. They can also determine whether the implementation complies with
the requirements of the architecture and, for example, where permissible
dependency rules have been adhered to.

6.6.1 Requirements and decision criteria

- Automatable, capable of being integrated into the build process
- Reporting, with processing of results in multiple formats (HTML, RSS, and so on), including visualization
- Flexible analysis criteria and metrics
- Support for multiple programming languages
- Definition of inclusion and exclusion criteria (i.e., which sections of the source code should be analyzed and how)

6.6.2 Challenges faced by static code analysis tools

- Support for multiple programming languages
- Dependencies and coupling arise in the source code as a result of either *direct* dependencies (calls, includes) or *indirect* dependencies (dependency injection, dependencies via data structures, or via the runtime environment). Indirect dependencies are considerably more difficult to analyze.

6.6.3 Examples

Static analysis:

- Application Intelligence Platform (CAST Software .Inc)
- Coverity (Synopsys)
- FindBugs (open source)
- Fortify Static Code Analyzer (Micro Focus)
- JDepend (open source)
- SonarQube (SonarSource)
- Sonargraph (hello2morrow GmbH)
- Sotograph (hello2morrow GmbH)
- structure101 (Headway Software)

6.7 Dynamic analysis tools

Dynamic analysis tools examine the runtime behavior of software. By analyzing and comparing running programs they can help developers to identify issues and understand processes.

The aims of dynamic analysis include:

Speed measurement
Time measurement of specific system components in relation to others
Measurement of memory usage
Statistical analysis (How often are individual system components used?)

6.7.1   Requirements and decision criteria

Minimum possible impact on runtime behavior, memory requirements, and CPU use
Comprehensible presentation of results, appropriate for the target group
Also suitable for distributed systems

6.7.2   Challenges faced by dynamic analysis tools

The measurement itself influences the system (known analogously in physics as the Heisenberg uncertainty principle). This is particularly evident in concurrent systems or processes.
The data produced by dynamic analysis soon becomes incomprehensible due to the sheer volume involved.

6.7.3   Examples

AppDynamics (AppDynamics, Inc.)
IBM Security AppScan (IBM)
JBoss Profiler (JBoss Community)
JProfiler (ej-technologies)
JRat (open source)
Jtest (Parasoft)
Perf4J (open source)

6.8   Build management tools

Build management tools enable versioning automation, compilation, packaging, testing, and inspection tasks for source code and associated artifacts.

These include:

Management of translation and transformation tasks (compile, link, deploy)

Continuous integration management
Dependency management (see Section 6.9)
Execution of and reporting on automated tests
Checking for compliance with structural specifications and programming conventions

6.8.1 Requirements and decision criteria

Build process definable (i.e., the steps necessary for the build can be defined on a system-specific basis)
Minimal dissolution of transitive dependencies (i.e., the absolute minimum necessary number of files are retranslated or relinked in a build run)
Integration with version and configuration management tools, code analysis, execution of automated tests and their associated reporting
Interface with continuous integration tools and processes
Support for different programming languages and tools
The speed at which the build processes run

6.8.2 Challenges faced by build management tools

Build management for large systems is resource intensive
The description/definition of builds needs to be synchronized with the decisions in the deployment view
There is currently no established standard syntax/language for build descriptions. Most build tools use their own language/syntax.
Systems are constructed using multiple programming languages (polyglot programming) with a mixture of compiled and interpreted systems

6.8.3 Examples

Apache Ant (build tool, primarily used for Java systems, task description using XML)
Apache Buildr (build system for many Java VM languages)
Apache Ivy (support for Java builds that enables subsequent loading of specific versions of required libraries from repositories)
Apache Maven (build tool for a wide range of build tasks, specifies conventions for directory and file structures, definition using hierarchically organized XML files)
Gant or Gradle (Ant equivalents in Groovy)

Make, NMake (the original tools in this category)
Rake (Make tool for Ruby)
Team Foundation Server (Microsoft commercial build and code management)

6.9   Configuration and version management tools

A configuration management tool primarily supports the software architect in the following tasks:

Assignment and selection of configuration elements
Inventorying
Configuration reconstruction

6.9.1   Requirements and decision criteria

Scalability for large development teams
Handling of any variants (branches, versions)
Reliability and robustness
Integration with other tools (e.g., version management, issue and requirements management, build tools, code management)

6.9.2   Challenges faced by configuration and version management tools

Fundamental terms and concepts of configuration and version management are often dependent on the tool used
Operations such as branching or merging are often complex in large systems, and are still prone to error, in spite of tool support. It is practically impossible to merge non-text artifacts (diagrams, models, binary files) from different branches.
Strategies for staging, transitions between development, test and operational environments, rights assignment between these environments and similar organizational responsibilities are complex tasks for which there are no standard solutions.
Comprehensibility (greater complexity results in more errors in the handling of configurations or versions)

6.9.3 Examples

- Tools for versioning of source code and files, such as CVS, Subversion, Git or Mercurial
- Tools for managing different versions of all artifacts in the development process and their dependencies—for example, Apache Ivy, Maven/Nexus
- Rational ClearCase (IBM Rational)
- OMNITRACKER (OMNINET GmbH)
- Perforce (Perforce Software)
- Surround SCM (Seapine)
- Team Foundation Server (Microsoft)

6.10 Code management tools

Code management tools support architects and developers in the creation, editing, and comprehension of source code. (Version and configuration management are addressed in Section 6.9.)

This category of tools includes:

- Syntax-based editors
- Refactoring tools for restructuring source code while retaining its functional characteristics
- Debuggers (see also Sections 6.6 and 6.7)
- Integrated development environments

6.10.1 Challenges faced by code management tools

- Stability when faced with large code bases (many and large files)
- Support for different programming languages (including mixed languages)
- Integration of build and deployment tools
- Integration of test tools

6.10.2 Examples

- Eclipse (open source IDE for Java and other languages, primarily those based on the Java platform, but also C++, Erlang, Prolog and others; flexible extension via plug-ins)
- IntelliJ (available as an open source and commercial IDE, extendible for many languages and via plug-ins)

NetBeans (open source IDE for Java and other Java-based languages; flexible extension via plug-ins)

Visual Studio (Microsoft development environment for Windows operating systems)

xCode (Apple development environment for Mac OS and iOS)

6.11   Testing tools

Automated unit and integration tests provide software architects and developers with early feedback on the structure and internal interfaces of their
building blocks and how they collaborate with each other. Tests are often the
first users of newly created building blocks, and can provide valuable information on their creation, evolution, and improvement. Unit and integration
test tools form part of:

Unit tests (for example, xUnit derivatives)

Runtime tests (for example, load/performance tests, stress tests, robustness
tests)

Penetration tests, attack scenarios

Management of test cases, test data, and test results

6.11.1   Requirements and decision criteria

Integration into the development environment

Simple, executable description of tests

Reporting of test results

Collection of test results from multiple test runs for identification of trends

6.11.2   Challenges faced by test tools

Support for heterogeneous or distributed systems

Synchronous management of test cases and their associated test data (a
version and configuration management task)

Automatic testing of user interfaces

Mocking (simulation) of external systems required for testing that are
not yet available (or cannot be used) as real systems. Support for a mock
frameworks category has become established.

6.11.3 Examples

An extensive overview is available at *http://www.opensourcetesting.org*.

- xUnit frameworks (all open source) for unit tests
- Acceptance test tools (FitNess, Cucumber, Spock)

6.12 Documentation tools

Documentation tools are intended to support software architects and developers in the long-term communication of decisions, structures, concepts, and other information. This tool category includes text-based and graphical tools for developing, maintaining, and generating documents.

6.12.1 Requirements and decision criteria

- Suitability for user groups/project teams
- Comparison of different document versions or statuses
- Integration with version and configuration management
- Compliance of the final documents with company or organization standards (for example, with corporate layout or corporate design)
- Ability to generate stakeholder-specific documentation
- Simple synchronization of documentation with releases or versions of the software
- Integration with bug- or issue-tracking systems

6.12.2 Challenges faced by documentation tools

- Version management
- Multiuser capability, in particular conflict handling (simple source code operations such as diff or merge present a major problem for most text processing systems)
- Generation of results for specific target groups in printed and electronic formats. Such considerations include layout and format requirements (such as corporate identity or corporate design), automatic generation of tables of contents and keyword indexes, compliance with documentation standards.
- Avoiding redundancy. It is essential that all information can be maintained in a single location. The transition from source code through models

(diagrams) to documentation is still tricky, but so-called "single-source" approaches are attempting to remedy the issue.

6.12.3 Examples

- Classic text processing ("office" products) from various vendors
- Markup-based approaches (DocBook, DITA, SGML, MarkDown, Textile, XHTML) that embed formatting and semantic information in text using special characters/strings
- Wikis (there are many open source wikis such as TWiki, Mediawiki, and TiddlyWiki (offline-capable)
- Confluence Team Collaboration (Atlassian)
- Many modeling tools can generate documentation from their database/repository.

6.13 Test your knowledge

Here are some detailed excerpts from the *Tools for software architects* section of the iSAQB curriculum [isaqb curriculum] to help you consolidate what you have learned.

- LG 5-1: Name and explain important tool categories.

  Ability to list and explain the most important categories of tools and their strengths and weaknesses with regard to the work of software architects

- LG 5-2: Select tools according to requirements.

  Software architects' work environment and tools depend on the respective conditions, constraints, and influencing factors

Appendix

A   Sample Questions

To gain an impression of the type of questions you can expect in an examination for the *iSAQB Certified Professional for Software Architecture (CPSA), Foundation Level*, we have provided some sample questions for you here. These examples do not claim to be compliant with the curriculum and are not identical to any real questions.

A.1   Excerpts from the examination regulations

In accordance with the current iSAQB examination regulations (*https:// www.isaqb.org/wp-content/uploads/2017/11/iSAQB_CPSA_Foundation_ Examination_Guide_EN_1.5.pdf*) the examination is comprised of 40–50 multiple choice questions. They need to be answered within a 75 minute time frame (earlier submission possible). Their value ranges from 1–3 points, depending on the level of difficulty; the total points possible for each question are shown in the question header. The general principle is: correct answers result in additional points, incorrect answers in subtracted points. The assessment is detailed below under "Types of Questions". The total score is 69 points.

To successfully pass the exam, the participant must achieve a minimum of 60% of the total score (at least 41.4 points).

No aids, tools or resources (like training material, books, telephones etc.) are allowed during the exam. In case the participant uses notepads or additional sheets of paper besides the official exam paper, he/she must leave them in the room at the end of the examination.

The participant is not allowed to leave the room during the examination.

Notification of Examination Outcome and Re-examination:

The participants will be notified of the outcome of the examination by the certifying body in written form. The certificate will be shipped by the certifying body to the participants' home address.

The examination fee must to be paid in full for the certificate to be sent. The examination can be retaken twice without a waiting period. In case of a third failure, the examination can be retaken after a waiting period of one year.

Types of Questions:

Please note that the examiners don't look for most appropriate answers, they only check for correct answers! It is possible that other answers are also correct but less appropriate. There are currently three different types of questions:

Type A
Single-selection questions. There is only one correct or one incorrect answer.

Type P
Multiple-selection questions. The number of correct answers specified in the text of the task must be selected from a list of possible answers.

Type K
Clarification questions. In this case the answer has to be selected from two possible options.

A.2   Sample Questions

Sample Questions on the topic *Basic concepts of software architectures*

Which architecture levels are there?
Choose the three most suitable from the following four answers.
A) *Module architecture*
B) *Infrastructure architecture*
C) *Business architecture*
D) *Business process architecture*

Which are the preconditions for creating software architecture?
Choose the two most suitable from the following four answers.
A) *A programming language should be chosen*
B) *The quality attributes should be known*
C) *The influencing factors should be known*
D) *The requirements must be complete and consistent*

Sample Questions on the topic *Design and development of software architectures*

Which factors can influence the design of software architectures?
Choose the three most suitable from the following four answers.
A) *Political*
B) *Organizational*
C) *Ethical*
D) *Technical*

Which are examples of usage types or categories of software systems?
Choose the three most suitable from the following four answers.
A) *Linnaeus' system*
B) *Interactive online system*
C) *Operational system*
D) *Real-time system*

Sample Questions on the topic *Description and communication of software architectures*

Which architecturals views might be used in the communication of software architectures?		
Assign all answers.		

false	true	
		A) *In case of separate focus, individual aspects of building blocks such as data view or interfaces can be defined as special view types.*
		B) *System context diagram*
		C) *Runtime view*
		D) *Building block view*

Which statements concerning the view concept in the software architecture are correct?	
Choose the three most suitable from the following four answers.	
	A) *It models (abstracts) the reality*
	B) *An individual view cannot represent the whole complexity of the system*
	C) *It reduces the complexity of representation*
	D) *To represent the system, two of the four shown views are sufficient*

Sample Questions on the topic *Software Architectures and Quality*

What are quality models?	
Choose the three most suitable from the following four answers.	
	A) *Quality models specify criteria for metrics to measure software quality.*
	B) *Quality models break down software quality into individual criteria.*
	C) *Quality models are needed to find the right evaluation method.*
	D) *Quality models describe software quality by providing sub terms.*

Name two well-known quality models.	
Choose the two most suitable from the following four answers.	
	A) *FURPS*
	B) *Model of Barbara Liskov*
	C) *GURPS*
	D) *Model of Boehm*

B List of Abbreviations

ANSA	Advanced Networked Systems Architecture
API	Application Programming Interface
ATAM	Architecture Tradeoff Analysis Method
BPMN	Business Process Model and Notation
CoCoME	Common Component Modeling Example
CORBA	Common Object Request Broker Architecture
CPSA	Certified Professional for Software Architecture
CPSA-F	Certified Professional for Software Architecture – Foundation Level
DDD	Domain Driven Design
DoDAF	Department of (US) Defense Architectural Framework
DSL	Domain-specific Language
EPC	Event-driven process chain
ER	Entity Relationship
FMC	Fundamental Modeling Concepts
FURPS	Acronym representing a model for classifying software quality attributes: Functionality, Usability, Reliability, Performance, Supportability
GoF	Gang of Four
GUI	Graphical User Interface
iSAQB	International Software Architecture Qualification Board
JDBC	Java Database Connectivity
JET	Java Emitter Templates
JRE	Java Runtime Environment
MDA	Model Driven Architecture
MDSD	Model Driven Software Development
MOF	Meta Object Facility
MVC	Model View Controller
MVP	Model View Presenter
OMG	Object Management Group
OMG-MDA	Model Driven Architecture of the Object Management Group

PAC	Presentation Abstraction Control
PIM	Platform Independent Model
PSM	Platform Specific Model
QoS	Quality of Service
RMI	Remote Method Invocation
RM-ODP	Reference Model of Open Distributed Processing
SAGA	Standards and Architectures for e-Government Applications, developed under for the German Federal Ministry of the Interior (BMI)
SEI	The Carnegie Mellon University Software Engineering Institute
SOA	Service-Oriented Architecture
TOGAF	The Open Group Architecture Framework
UML	Unified Modeling Language
XSLT	Extensible Stylesheet Language Transformation

C Glossary[1]

Term	Explanation/Definition	Source
Adapter (pattern)	A design pattern: Adapts the interface of a class to another interface expected by its users. The adapter pattern enables collaboration by classes that otherwise would not be able to collaborate due to incompatible interfaces. A comparable example from day-to-day life: An adapter that enables connection of the different types of power outlets used in Europe and the USA.	[GHJ94]
Aggregation	A special case of a relationship or association. An "Is part of" or a "Consists of" relationship exists between the involved elements. See →Composition, →Association, →Relationship.	[Bal00]
arc42	A freely available template for describing and documenting software architectures	
Architectural decision	A decision that sustainably or fundamentally impacts →structures, concepts, implementation, and the like. Example: A decision that impacts the database technology or the technical foundations of the user interface.	
Architectural description	An architectural description consists of a number of architecture levels. An architecture level combines a number of views to form a descriptive element.	Chapter 2
Architectural (architecture) pattern	"An architectural pattern expresses a fundamental structural organization schema for software systems. It provides a set of predefined subsystems, specifies their responsibilities, and includes rules and guidelines for organizing the relationships between them" (Buschmann+1996, page 12). Similar to *Architecture style* Examples include: Model-View-Controller Layers Pipes-and-Filter CQRS	[BM++96]
Architectural style	The central architectural metaphor of the system	Chapter 2

---

1 The iSAQB Glossary of Software Architecture Terminology is available from Leanpub at: *https://leanpub.com/isaqbglossary/read.*

Term	Explanation/Definition	Source
Architecture goal	(Syn: Architectural quality goal, Architectural quality requirement): A quality attribute that the system is required to fulfill. The quality attribute is understood to be an architectural issue. The architecture needs to be designed in a way that fulfills this architectural goal. These goals often have *long-term character* in contrast to (short-term) project goals.	
Architecture view	A representation of a system from a specific viewpoint. Important and well-known views are: Context view Building block view Runtime view Deployment view	Chapter 2
Artifact	Tangible by-product created or generated during development of software. Examples of artifacts are use cases, all kinds of diagrams, UML models, requirements and design documents, source code, test cases, class-files, archives.	
Association	Models links between objects (generally speaking, between →Building blocks). Each association can be described in more detail using →Cardinalities and (role) names. →Relationship, →Dependency	[Bal00]
ATAM	Architecture Tradeoff Analysis Method. A scenario-based, qualitative evaluation method for software architectures, developed at the SEI.	[BCK03]
Black box	A view of a building block that hides its internal structure. Black boxes comply with the Input-Process-Output (IPO) model or pattern. Their minimum specification comprises defined input and output interfaces and a function. Optionally, a black box can also define non-functional characteristics (such as run times or quantities). →White box	
Blackboard (pattern)	One of the architectural patterns from [BM++96]. A set of independent building blocks collects information about a problem based on a common data structure (the blackboard). Each building block solves specific parts of the overall problem. The building blocks function independently; their approach depends on the current progress of the overall problem-solving process. Excerpt from [BM++96]: *"The Blackboard architectural pattern is useful for problems for which no deterministic solution strategies are known. Several specialized subsystems assemble their knowledge to build a (possibly) partial or approximate solution."*	[BM++96, p. 71]
Bottom-up approach	A concept that defines the "direction" of work when modeling and designing: starting from specific (specialized, detailed) elements and moving to abstract (general) elements. →Top-down	

Term	Explanation/Definition	Source
Broker (pattern)	An architectural pattern for structuring systems in which the component elements interact via service calls. Services register themselves with the broker, and the broker manages the communication between the clients (i.e., clients use services via the broker). Example: CORBA (Common Object Request Broker Architecture) Excerpt from [BM++96]: *"The Broker architectural pattern can be used to structure distributed software systems with decoupled components that interact by remote service invocations. A broker component is responsible for coordinating communication, such as forwarding requests, as well as for transmitting results and exceptions."*	[M++96, p. 99]
Building block	General or abstract term for all kinds of artifacts from which software is constructed. Part of the static structure (building block view) of software architecture. Building blocks can be hierarchically structured and may contain other (smaller) building blocks. Some examples of alternative names for building blocks are component, module, package, namespace, class, file, program, subsystem, function, configuration, data-definition.	Chapter 2
Building block view	Shows the static structure of the system and how its source code is organized. Usually hierarchical, starting from the context view. Complemented by one or more runtime scenarios.	
Business architecture	*"A blueprint of the enterprise that provides a common understanding of the organization and is used to align strategic objectives and tactical demands."* OMG Business Architecture Working Group See also →Enterprise IT architecture	
Cardinality	Denotes the valence of an →Association (i.e., it specifies the number of objects or building blocks involved in the →Association)	[Bal00]
Class diagram	A UML diagram in which classes, their attributes, operations and →Relationships (→Associations) with one another are depicted	
Cohesion	The degree to which elements of a building block, component, or module belong together. It measures the strength of the relationship between the individual pieces of functionality within a given component. In cohesive systems, functionality is strongly related. It is usually characterized as *high cohesion* or *low cohesion*. Always strive for high cohesion. High cohesion often implies good reusability, low coupling, and comprehensibility.	
Component	See →Building block. Structural element of an architecture.	
Component diagram	A UML diagram in which components, their (provided and required) interfaces, and the relationships between them are depicted	
Component view	An architecture view in which components and their relationships with one another are depicted. One possible notation is a UML2 component diagram.	

Term	Explanation/Definition	Source
Composition	Combination of simple elements (e.g., functions, data types, building blocks) to build more complicated, more powerful, or more functional ones. In UML: Contained elements are automatically destroyed with the owning element.	[Bal00]
Configuration management	Excerpt from [IEEE 610.12-1990]: *"A discipline applying technical and administrative direction and surveillance to identify and document the functional and physical characteristics of a configuration item, control changes to those characteristics, record and report change processing and implementation status, and verify compliance with specified requirements."*	[IEEE 610.12-1990]
Coupling	Coupling represents the type and degree of interdependence between software building blocks. It is a measure of how closely connected two components are. Always aim for as little coupling as possible. Coupling is usually contrasted with cohesion. Low coupling often correlates with high cohesion, and vice versa. Low coupling is a sign of a well-structured system. When combined with high cohesion, it supports comprehensibility and maintainability.	
Data type coupling	Coupling using common data types or structures	
DDD	→Domain-driven design	
Delegation	A building block delegates a task to another building block instead of carrying it out itself. See also →Dependency, →Relationship	
Dependency	See coupling	
Dependency injection	*Use* or *Include* relationships between building blocks are created at runtime by a dedicated component rather than by the corresponding building block itself. Well-known examples are Spring or Google Guice. See *http://martinfowler.com/articles/injection.html#FormsOfDependency Injection*	
Deployment view	An architectural view showing the technical infrastructure within which a system or artifacts will be deployed and executed. *"This view defines the physical environment in which the system is intended to run, including the hardware environment your system needs (e.g., processing nodes, network interconnections, and disk storage facilities), the technical environment requirements for each node (or node type) in the system, and the mapping of your software elements to the runtime environment that will execute them."* (as defined by Rozanski+2011)	

Term	Explanation/Definition	Source
Design principle	Set of guidelines that helps software developers to design and implement better solutions, where "better" means the avoidance of the following three *bad characteristics:* Rigidity: A system or element is difficult to change because every change potentially affects many other elements Fragility: When elements are changed, unexpected results, defects, or otherwise negative consequences occur in other elements Immobility: An element is difficult to reuse because it cannot be disentangled from the rest of the system These characteristics were formulated by Robert Martin, quoted from *OODesign.com*	[Mar03], [ES10]
DIN ISO/IEC 9126	ISO 9126 – Software Engineering – Product Quality. Describes, among other things, quality characteristics for software.	[ISO/ IEC 9126]
DIN ISO/IEC 25010	ISO 25010 – Systems and software engineering – Systems and software Quality Requirements and Evaluation (SQuaRE) – Systems and software quality models. Describes, among other things, quality characteristics for software.	[ISO/ IEC 25010]
Domain-driven design	Design and implementation of software systems on the basis of functional abstractions. DDD implements functionally motivated entities and services as the fundamental elements of the overall software architecture. In practice, DDD is used together with test-driven development.	[Eva04]
Dynamic view	An architecture view that describes the dynamic behavior of one or more building blocks. A dynamic view can, for example, describe the interaction of multiple building blocks in a specific use case scenario. →Runtime view	
Embedded system	Except from [GB03]: *"A combination of computer hardware and software, and perhaps additional mechanical or other parts, designed to perform a dedicated function."* Embedded systems contain software that is embedded into physical objects. With significant resource limitations in terms of the available hardware, they carry out tasks that are critical in terms of both data security and functional reliability, and which have to fulfill demanding functional and quality requirements. The functionality mostly involves regulation, control, or communication functions.	Chapter 2 [GB03]
Encapsulation	Encapsulation is a technique that comprises one or both of the following concepts: Restrict access to some of an object's components Bundle data with the methods or functions operating on that data Encapsulation is a mechanism for information hiding.	
Enterprise IT Architecture	Synonym: Enterprise Architecture. Structures and concepts for the IT systems support of an entire company. Atomic subjects in an enterprise architecture are individual software systems also referred to as "applications".	

Term	Explanation/Definition	Source
Facade	A facade is a design pattern from the *structure patterns* family. It provides a standardized and usually simplified interface to a set of interfaces in a subsystem. It distributes the functionality to other classes of the subsystem, thus simplifying subsystem use.	
FMC	Acronym ("Fundamental Modeling Concepts"). A graphical notation for system modeling. See *http://fmc-modeling.org*	
Functional requirement	Translated excerpt from [PR15]: *"A functional requirement defines a system function to be provided by that system or a component thereof."*	[PR15]
Gateway (pattern)	Excerpt from [Fow03]: *"An object that encapsulates access to an external system or resource."*	[Fow03, p. 466]
Hardware coupling	Coupling of software building blocks to the hardware on which the software is executed. For example, is created via direct access to the hardware from within a building block.	
Hardware/ software codesign	An approach to designing systems containing hardware and software building blocks. The design of the hardware and software takes place as an integrated process (i.e., no predefined or existing hardware platform is used. Instead, a breakdown into hardware and software is defined for the specific system, and hardware and software are designed based on this breakdown).	
Information hiding	Design principle: For a specific building block only the information necessary for correct use of that building block is provided (i.e., no implementation details, design decisions, or similar).	
Information system	The focus of information systems is on management and processing of information. Large amounts of data or complex data structures have to be managed, processed, evaluated, and calculated, and several thousand users may have to be served both simultaneously and interactively.	Chapter 2

Inheritance	Concept that enables subclasses of a defined class of objects to inherit the definitions, attributes, operations, and relations of one or more general classes.
	
	    Single inheritance: Inherit from only one other object
	
	    Multiple inheritance: May inherit from multiple objects
		[Bal00]

Interface	Boundary across which two building blocks interact or communicate with each other	Chapter 2
iSAQB	International Software Architecture Qualification Board. An association for standardization of the training of software architects. See *http://www.isaqb.org*	
ISO/IEC/IEE 42010:2011	ISO 42010: Systems and software engineering – Architecture description Defines a framework for describing architectures, viewpoints and views.	[ISO/ IEC/IEE 42010:2011]

Term	Explanation/Definition	Source
MDA	Model-Driven Architecture. An Object Management Group (OMG) standard for model-driven software development. OMG definition from the MDA Guide 2.0: *"MDA provides an approach for deriving value from models and architecture in support of the full life cycle of physical, organizational and I.T. systems[1]."* [1] *A "System", in this context, is any arrangement of parts and their interrelationships, working together as a whole. This is inclusive of designs at all levels such as an entire enterprise, a process, information structures or I.T. systems.* See *http://www.omg.org/mda/specs.htm*	[MDA Guide 2.0]
MDSD	Model-Driven Software Development. Translated excerpt from [RH06]: *"Model-driven software development is the term used for software development processes in which the focus is on models that can be used as self-contained development artifacts."*	[RH06]
Model	An abstract description of a system that contains all details of relevance to a specific problem	
Model-based development	See MDSD	
Modeling Tool	A tool that creates models (for example, UML or BPMN). Can be used to create consistent diagrams for documentation. Each model element exists only once but can be consistently displayed in many diagrams (as opposed to a simple drawing tool).	
Node	A processing resource (execution environment, processor, machine, virtual machine, application server) with which artifacts can be deployed and executed	
Non-functional requirement	A system development requirement that does not relate to the functionality of the system. Non-functional requirements often relate to quality characteristics or specify conditions for system development.	
Open/Closed principle	Excerpt from [Mey88]: *"... software entities (classes, modules, functions, etc.) should be open for extension, but closed for modification."*	[Mey88]
Package diagram	A UML diagram in which packages, package contents, and the dependencies and relationships between packages are depicted	
Prototype	A prototype represents a model of a planned product or component, usable for the corresponding purposes but often in a simplified form. It can correspond to the final product purely in terms of its appearance but also in technical terms. A prototype often serves as preparation for mass production, but can also be planned as a one-off item that is solely intended to demonstrate a specific concept. The prototype represents an important stage in the design and development process and is not only used in technical contexts.	

Term	Explanation/Definition	Source
Prototyping	(or Prototype construction). A method that offers swift results and early feedback on the suitability of a solution approach. Enables early identification of problems and requests for changes, and enables correction/implementation with less effort than would be necessary if they were not identified until after complete implementation of the software.	
Proxy (pattern)	The proxy is a design pattern from the *structure patterns* family. It shifts control of an object to an upstream surrogate object.	
Qualitative architecture evaluation	Evaluation of a system in terms of individual quality characteristics. For each of these characteristics a (normally subjective) evaluation is carried out to determine whether and to what extent the system fulfills the requirement characteristic or whether a risk of non-fulfillment exists.	
Quality (of software)	In [ISO/IEC 25010] the quality of a software product is described via quality characteristics such as maintainability or efficiency	[ISO/IEC 25010]

Quality attribute	Software quality is the degree to which a system possesses the desired combination of *attributes* (see: software quality).
	
	Important quality attributes are performance, robustness, security, safety, flexibility, dependability, maintainability, and so on. See also ISO-25010.
	
	It is helpful to distinguish between:
	  Runtime quality attributes (which can be observed at execution time of the system)
	  Non-runtime quality attributes (which cannot be observed while the system executes)
	  Business quality attributes (cost, schedule, marketability, appropriateness for the organization in question)
	
	Examples of runtime quality attributes are functionality, performance, security, availability, usability, and interoperability.
	
	Examples of non-runtime quality attributes are modifiability, portability, reusability, integratability, and testability.
		[DIN 55350-11, 1995-08, Nr. 5]

Quality model	A quality model operationalizes the concept of software quality via additional detailing and specifics. This takes place via derivation of sub-terms, thus creating a tree (or network) of terms and sub-terms.	
Relationship	Generic term denoting some kind of dependency between elements of an architecture. Different types of relationship are used within architectures—for example, calls, notifications, ownership, containment, creation, inheritance.	
Runtime View	Shows the cooperation or collaboration of building blocks (or instances of them) at runtime within specific scenarios. Should refer to elements of the →Building block view. Can (but doesn't have to) be expressed in the form of UML sequence or activity diagrams.	
Sequence diagram	UML diagram type. A graphical, time-based depiction of messages between objects and classes (with a vertical time axis). Messages are represented by horizontal lines, objects and classes by dashed vertical lines. Used for modeling runtime view scenarios.	[Bal00]

Term	Explanation/Definition	Source
Software	From [IEEE 610.12-1990]: *"Computer programs, procedures, and possibly associated documentation and data pertaining to the operation of a computer system."*	[IEEE-610.12-1990]
Software architecture	From [ISO/IEC/IEEE 42010:2011]: *"The fundamental organization of a system embodied in its components, their relationships to each other, and to the environment, and the principles guiding its design and evolution."* A software architecture defines the fundamental principles and rules for the organization of a system, its structuring into building blocks and interfaces, and the relationships of the building blocks and interfaces with each other and the surrounding environment. It thus defines guidelines for the entire system lifecycle, from analysis through design and implementation to operation and enhancement. It also defines guidelines for the development and operating organization.	[ISO/IEC/IEEE 42010: 2011] Chapter 2
Software-intensive system	A collection of building blocks organized so that it accomplishes the planned purpose of the system. Building blocks that consist entirely or for the most part of software carry out essential tasks for accomplishment of the system's purpose. The software element of the system consists of a collection of programs, procedures, data, and associated documentation.	Chapter 2
Software quality	Translated excerpt from [Bal00]: *"Software quality is the entirety of the characteristics and characteristic values of a software product that affect its fitness to fulfill defined or demanded requirements."* This definition relates solely to product quality but not to process quality.	[Bal00]
Stakeholder	A stakeholder is an individual or a group with an interest in the course or result of a process or project. Stakeholders (project participants) are all persons, institutions and, documents affected in any way by the development and operation of a system. This also includes persons who do not play a part in the development of a system but who, for example, use or maintain the new system or provide training for it. Stakeholders are the providers of information for objectives, requirements and conditions that apply to the system or product in development.	
Scenario	1. An exemplary sequence within a system. A sequence of processing steps. Extensive tasks or processes can be documented by a set of scenarios. 2. Evaluation scenario	[Bal00]
System	A part of the real or theoretical world, consisting of subsystems (building blocks, partial systems, components) that can have various relationships to one another. From [IEEE 610.12-1990]: *"A collection of components organized to accomplish a specific function or set of functions."*	[Bal00] [IEEE 610.12-1990]
TOGAF	The Open Group Architecture Framework. A framework for Enterprise Architecture. See *http://www.opengroup.org/togaf*	

Term	Explanation/Definition	Source
Top-down approach	A concept that defines the "direction" of work when modeling and designing. Starting from abstract (general, high-level) elements and moving to specific (detailed) elements. →Bottom-up	
UML	Unified Modeling Language. A graphical modeling language for the specification, design, and documentation of software components and other systems. Managed and developed by the Object Management Group (OMG), standardized by OMG and, for Version 2.1.2, ISO (ISO/IEC 19505).	
Utility tree	A methodical tool for defining quality requirements. The "root" of the (quality attributes) utility tree is formed by the term "Quality", while the "branches" are quality attributes/characteristics (hierarchically refined where necessary). The "leaves" depict scenarios and concrete descriptions of individual quality requirements.	
View	→Architecture view. A representation of a system from the viewpoint of specific concerns.	
White box (white box view)	Depicts the internal structure of a system or building block in the form of black boxes and their interrelationships, and the external interfaces of the building block. →Black box	

D References

This overview contains German- and English-language references. These are referenced in both the German and English curricula. German references are denoted using the [DE] addendum.

[ARC42] The arc42 Template. *https://arc42.org/.*

[Bal00] [DE] Balzert, H.: Lehrbuch der Software-Technik – Software-Entwicklung. 2. Aufl., Spektrum Akademischer Verlag, Heidelberg, 2000.

[BCK03] Bass, L.; Clements, P.; Kazmann, R.: Software Architecture in Practice. 2nd ed., Addison-Wesley Professional, 2003.

[BJ+06] [DE] Broy, M. et al.: Dagstuhl-Manifest zur Strategischen Bedeutung des Software Engineering in Deutschland. Dagstuhl Seminar Proceedings, 2006. *http://drops.dagstuhl.de/opus/volltexte/2006/585.*

[BM00] [DE] Bundesministerium für Bildung und Forschung (BMBF): Analyse und Evaluation der Softwareentwicklung in Deutschland, 2000. *https://www.iese.fraunhofer.de/content/dam/iese/de/documents/ Softwareentwicklung_Deutschland_Evasoft_tcm122-7431.pdf.*

[BM++96] Buschmann, F.; Meunier, R.; Rohnert, H.; Sommerlad, P.: A System of Patterns: Pattern-Oriented Software Architecture, Volume 1. John Wiley & Sons, 1996.

[BW97] Buchi, M.; Weck, W.: A Plea for Gray-Box Components. Turku Centre for Computer Science, 1997.

[CB++10] Clements, P.; Bachmann, F.; Bass, L.; Garlan, D.; Ivers, J.; Little, R.; Merson, P.; Nord, R.; Stafford, J.: Documenting Software Architectures: Views and Beyond. 2nd ed., Addison-Wesley, 2010.

[CKH05] [DE] Conrad, S.; Koschel, A., Hasselbring, W.: Enterprise Application Integration. Spektrum Akademischer Verlag, Heidelberg, 2005.

[CKK02] Clements, P.; Kazman, R.; Klein, M.: Evaluating Software Architectures – Methods and Case Studies. Addison-Wesley Professional, 2002.

[**Clem03**] Clements, P.: Documenting software architectures: views and beyond. Addison- Wesley, 2003.

[**CoCoME**] Modelling Contest: Common Component Modelling Example (CoCoME). GI-Dagstuhl Research Seminar. *http://www.cocome.org.*

[**DE++09**] [DE] Dunkel, J.; Eberhardt, A.; Fischer, F.; Kleiner, C.; Koschel, A.: Systemarchitekturen für Verteilte Anwendungen, Hanser Verlag, München, 2009.

[**Die00**] [DE] Diethelm, G.: Projektmanagement, Bd. 1: Grundlagen. NW Verlag, Berlin, 2000.

[**Dij72**] Dijkstra, E. W.: The humble programmer. Communications of the ACM CACM, Vol. 15, Issue 10, Oct., pp. 859–866, 1972.

[**D'SW98**] D'Souza, D. F.: Objects, Components, and Frameworks with UML: The Catalysis Approach. Addison-Wesley Professional, 1998.

[**Dum01**] [DE] Dumke, R.: Software Engineering: Eine Einführung für Informatiker und Ingenieure. 3. Aufl., Vieweg, Braunschweig, Wiesbaden, 2001.

[**Eel05**] Eeles, P.: Capturing Architectural Requirements, IBM, 2005. *http://www.ibm.com/developerworks/rational/library/4706.html.*

[**EH+08**] [DE] Engels, G.; Hess, A.; Humm, B.; Juwig, O.: Quasar Enterprise – Anwendungslandschaften serviceorientiert gestalten. dpunkt.verlag, Heidelberg, 2008.

[**EK08**] El Emam, K.; Koru, A. G.: A Replicated Survey of IT Software Project Failures. IEEE Software, Vol. 25, No. 5, pp. 84–90, 2008.

[**ES10**] [DE] Eilebrecht, K.; Starke, G.: Patterns kompakt: Entwurfsmuster für effektive Software-Entwicklung. 3. Aufl., Spektrum Akademischer Verlag, Heidelberg, 2010.

[**EV10**] Eveleens, J. L.; Verhoef, C.: The Rise and Fall of the Chaos Report Figures. IEEE Software, Vol. 27, No. 1, pp. 30–36, 2010.

[**Eva04**] Evans, E.: Domain Driven Design. Addison-Wesley, 2004. *http://dddcommunity.org/book/evans_2003/.*

[**Fow99**] Fowler, M.: Refactoring – Improving the Design of Existing Code. Addison-Wesley, 1999.

[**Fow03**] Fowler, M.: Patterns of Enterprise Application Architecture. Addison-Wesley, Boston, 2003.

[**GB03**] Ganssle, J.; Barr, M.: Embedded Systems Dictionary. 2003.

[**GEM04**] Grünbacher, P.; Egyed, A.; Medvidovic, N.: Reconciling software requirements and architectures with intermediate models. Software and System Modeling 3(3), pp. 235–253, 2004.

[GHJ94] Gamma, E.; Helm, R.; Johnson, R. E.: Design Patterns. Elements of Reusable Object-Oriented Software. Addison-Wesley Longman, Amsterdam, 1994.

[HM+07] Herold, S.; Metzger, A.; Stallbaum, H.; Rausch, A.: Towards Bridging the Gap between Goal-Oriented Requirements Engineering and Compositional Architecture Development. Proc. of the Second Workshop on Sharing and Reusing Architectural Knowledge – Architecture, Rationale, and Design Intent. ICSE 2007, Minneapolis, May 2007.

[HNS99] Hofmeister, C.; Nord, R.; Soni, D.: Applied Software Architecture. Addison-Wesley Professional, 1999.

[HS11] [DE] Hruschka P.; Starke, G.: arc42 – Ressourcen für Software-Architekten, 2011. *http://www.arc42.de*.

[isaqb-curriculum] International Software Architecture Qualification Board e. V. (iSAQB), Downloads Documents. *https://www.isaqb.org/wp-content/ uploads/2017/11/isaqb-Curriculum-foundation-v4-1-1-2017-EN_new.pdf*.

[isaqb-PuB_2017] Examination Rules and Examples – Certified Professional for Software Architecture Foundation Level. International Software Architecture Qualification Board e. V., Version: 1.5. 2017-11-27. *https://www.isaqb.org/wp-content/uploads/2017/11/iSAQB_CPSA_ Foundation_Examination_Guide_EN_1.5.pdf*.

[Kru95] Kruchten, P.: Architectural Blueprints – The "4+1" View Model of Software Architecture. IEEE Software 12 (6), Nov., pp. 42–50, 1995.

[Lit05] [DE] Litke, H.-D. (Hrsg.): Projektmanagement – Handbuch für die Praxis. Hanser Verlag, München, 2005.

[Mar03] Martin, R.C.: Agile Software Development, Principles, Patterns, and Practices. Pearson Education, Upper Saddle River, 2003.

[May05] [DE] Mayr, H.: Projekt Engineering: Ingenieurmäßige Softwareentwicklung in Projektgruppen. 2. Aufl., Fachbuchverlag, Leipzig, 2005.

[McC76] McCabe, T. J.: A Complexity Measure. IEEE Transactions on Software Engineering, Vol. SE-2, pp. 308–320, 1976.

[MDA Guide 2.0] Object Management Group: Model Driven Architecture (MDA): The MDA Guide rev. 2.0, *http://www.omg.org/mda*.

[Mey88] Meyer, B.: Object Oriented Software Construction. Prentice Hall, 1988.

[MRW77] McCall, J. A.; Richards, P.K.; Walters, G. F.: Factors in Software Quality, Vol. I–III, Rome Air Development Centre. Technical Report, New York, 1977.

[NSPE] NSPE Code of Ethics for Engineers. *http://www.nspe.org/Ethics/CodeofEthics/index.html*.

[Nus01] Nuseibeh, B.: Weaving the Software Development Process Between Requirements and Architecture. Proc. of ICSE 2001 Workshop STRAW-01, Toronto, May 2001.

[OS13] [DE] Oestereich, B.; Scheithauer, A.: Analyse und Design mit UML 2.5: Objektorientierte Softwareentwicklung. 11. Aufl., Oldenbourg Verlag, München, 2013.

[O'RF+03] O'Rourke, C.; Fishman, N.; Selkow, W.: Enterprise Architecture Using the Zachman Framework. Course Technology, 2003.

[PR15] Pohl, K.; Rupp, C.: Requirements Engineering Fundamentals: A Study Guide for the Certified Professional for Requirements Engineering Exam - Foundation Level - IREB compliant. 2nd ed., Rocky Nook, San Rafael, CA, 2015.

[Reu12] Reuters, T.: Web of Knowledge. *www.knowledge.reuters.com.*

[RH06] [DE] Reussner, R.; Hasselbring, W. (Hrsg.): Handbuch der Software-Architektur, dpunkt.verlag, Heidelberg, 2006.

[RM-ODP] RM-ODP Wiki. *https://en.wikipedia.org/wiki/RM-ODP.*

[RQ+12] [DE] Rupp, C.; Queins, S.: UML 2 glasklar: Praxiswissen für die UML-Modellierung. 4. Aufl., Hanser Verlag, München, 2012.

[RR++08] Rausch, A.; Reussner, R.; Mirandola, R.; Plásil, F.: The Common Component Modeling Example. LNCS 5153, Springer-Verlag, Heidelberg, Berlin, 2008.

[SAGA08] [DE] Standards und Architekturen für E-Government-Anwendungen (SAGA), Bundesministerium des Innern (BMI), Version 4.0, Stand: März 2008.

[SD00] [DE] Siedersleben, J.; Denert, E.: Wie baut man Informationssysteme? Überlegungen zur Standardarchitektur. Informatik Spektrum, Vol. 23, No. 4, S. 247–257, 2000. *http://www.springerlink.com/content/jdfaxdb44n15levh.*

[SEI Def] Software Architecture, Community Software Architecture Definitions. *http://www.sei.cmu.edu/architecture/start/glossary/community.cfm.*

[Sie03] [DE] Siedersleben, J. (Hrsg.): Quasar: Die sd&m Standardarchitektur, Teil I. *https://docplayer.org/19346553-Quasar-quasar-die-sd-m-standardarchitektur-teil-1-johannes-siedersleben-hrsg.html.*

[Sie04] [DE] Siedersleben, J.: Moderne Softwarearchitektur – Umsichtig planen, robust bauen mit Quasar. dpunkt.verlag, Heidelberg, 2004.

[Sta15] [DE] Starke, G.: Effektive Softwarearchitekturen: Ein praktischer Leitfaden. 7. Aufl., Hanser Verlag, München, 2015.

[Sta99] Standish Group International, Inc.: CHAOS: A Recipe for Success, 1999.

[**SV99**] Sharipo, C.; Varian, H. R.: Information Rules. A Strategic Guide to the Network Economy. Harvard Business School Press, Boston, Mass., 1999.

[**Szy98**] Szyperski, C.: Component Software: Beyond Object-oriented Programming. Addison-Wesley Longman, Amsterdam, 1998.

[**TOGAF**] TOGAF Version 9.2 "Enterprise Edition". *http://www.opengroup.org/togaf*.

[**TT+00**] Tapscott, D.; Ticoll, D.; Lowry, A.: Digital Capital. Harnessing the Power of Business Webs. Harvard Business School Press, Boston, Mass., 2000.

[**UML-1a**] UML-Specification: *http://www.omg.org/technology/documents/formal/uml.htm*.

[**UML-1b**] Object Management Group (OMG), UML 2.3 Infrastructure Specification, 2010. *http://www.omg.org/spec/UML/2.3/Infrastructure/PDF*.

[**UML-1c**] Object Management Group (OMG), UML 2.3 Superstructure Specification, 2010. *http://www.omg.org/spec/UML/2.3/Superstructure/PDF*.

[**VA++09**] [DE] Vogel, O.; Arnold, I.; Chughtai, A.; Ihler, E.; Kehrer, T.; Mehlig, U.; Zdun, D.: Software-Architektur, Grundlagen – Konzepte – Praxis. 2. Aufl., Spektrum Akademischer Verlag, Heidelberg, 2009.

[**Vit60**] Vitruvius: The Ten Books on Architecture. Dover Publications, 1960.

Websites

www.ireb.org International Requirements Engineering Board e.V. (IREB)

www.isaqb.org International Software Architecture Qualification Board e.V. (iSAQB)

www.istqb.org International Software Testing Qualifications Board (ISTQB)

www.pmi.org Project Management Institute (PMI)

Standards and Norms

[**DIN 55350-11:2008-05**] DIN 55350-11:2008-05– Concepts for quality management - Part 11: Supplement to DIN EN ISO 9000:2005.

[**DIN 66272, 1994-10**] DIN 66272, 1994-10 – Information technology – Software product evaluation – Quality characteristics and guidelines for their use.

[**IEEE 610.12-1990**] IEEE Standard Glossary of Software Engineering Terminology, *http://standards.ieee.org/findstds/standard/610.12-1990.html*.

[**ISO/IEC 9126**] ISO/IEC 9126-1:2001 Software engineering – Product quality – Part 1: Quality model (identical with [DIN 66272, 1994-10], Information technology – Software product evaluation – Quality characteristics and guidelines for their use).

ISO/IEC TR 9126-2:2003 Software engineering – Product quality – Part 2: External metrics.
ISO/IEC TR 9126-3:2003 Software engineering – Product quality – Part 3: Internal metrics.

[ISO/IEC 25010] ISO/IEC 25010:2011 Systems and software engineering – Systems and software Quality Requirements and Evaluation (SQuaRE) – System and software quality models.

[ISO/IEC/IEEE 42010:2011] ISO/IEC/IEEE 42010:2011 – Systems and software engineering – Architecture description.

Index

Printed in the USA
CPSIA information can be obtained
at www.ICGtesting.com
JSHW051457221024
72172JS00010B/92

9 783864 906251